Collins

Aiming for Level
Reading

6

Caroline Bentley-Davies

Gareth Calway

Nicola Copitch

Steve Eddy

Najoud Ensaff

Matthew Tett

Series editor: Gareth Calway

William Collins' dream of knowledge for all began with the publication of his first book in 1819. A self-educated mill worker, he not only enriched millions of lives, but also founded a flourishing publishing house. Today, staying true to this spirit, Collins books are packed with inspiration, innovation and practical expertise. They place you at the centre of a world of possibility and give you exactly what you need to explore it.

Collins. Freedom to teach.

Published by Collins
An imprint of HarperCollins Publishers
77–85 Fulham Palace Road
Hammersmith
London
W6 8JB

Browse the complete Collins catalogue at
www.collinseducation.com

10 9 8 7
ISBN 978 0 00 731358 7

Caroline Bentley-Davies, Gareth Calway, Nicola Copitch, Steve Eddy, Najoud Ensaff and Matthew Tett assert their moral rights to be identified as the authors of this work.

British Library Cataloguing in Publication Data.
A Catalogue record for this publication is available from the British Library.

Commissioned by Catherine Martin
Design and typesetting by Jordan Publishing Design
Cover Design by Angela English
Printed and bound by Martins the Printers

With thanks to Mike Gould, Jill Thraves, Gemma Wain and Jo Kemp.

Acknowledgements

The publishers gratefully acknowledge the permissions granted to reproduce the copyright material in this book. While every effort has been made to trace and contact copyright holders, where this has not been possible the publishers will be pleased to make the necessary arrangements at the first opportunity.

Extract from rivieratravel.co.uk (p6); extract by R. Bentley-Davies (p6); extract from 'Preludes' T.S. Eliot, published by Faber & Faber (p8); extract from 'Friday Night at the Royal Station Hotel' by Philip Larkin, in High Windows, published by Faber & Faber (p9); extract from The First Four Minutes by Sir Roger Bannister, published by Sutton Publishing (p10); extract from Screw It, Let's Do It, Expanded by Richard Branson, published by Virgin Books (p11); extract from an article in The Times by David Brown, © The Times and NI Syndication 2009 (p12); extract from an article in The Daily Telegraph by Gordon Rayner © The Telegraph Group 2009 (p14); 'Early Bird Blues' by Sophie Hannah, from Essential Poems, edited by Daisy Goodwin, published by HarperCollins Publishers (p18); 'Symptoms' by Sophie Hannah © Sophie Hannah (p20); extracts from Stone Cold by Robert Swindells, published by Puffin Books, part of Penguin Books Ltd. (pp22, 23); extracts from 'The Boys' Toilets' by Robert Westall, in Ghost Stories, published by Kingfisher, part of Pan Macmillan (pp24, 25); extracts from 'Nothing to be Afraid Of' by Jan Mark, in Funny Stories, chosen by Michael Rosen, published by Kingfisher, a part of Pan Macmillan (pp26, 27); extract from 'The Hour and the Man' by R. Barr (p30), extract from 'The Secret of City Cemetery' by P. Bone (p30), extract from 'The Davenport' by J. Ritchie (p31), extract from 'The Talking Head' by R. Scott (p31) from The Young Oxford Book of Nasty Endings I, edited by Dennis Pepper, published by Oxford University Press; extract from 'Rendezvous' by Daniel Ransom, in From Beginning to End, edited by Mike Royston, published by Heinemann (p31); articles from Cosmo Girl online, © Hearst Communications (pp32,33); extracts from The Play of The Secret Diary of Adrian Mole, aged 13 ¾ by Sue Townsend, published by Heinemann (pp34, 35); extract from The Other Side of Truth by Beverley Naidoo, published by Puffin Books, part of Penguin Books Ltd. (p36); 'Like Mother, Like Son' by Pauline Cartledge, in From Beginning to End, edited by Mike Royston, published by Heinemann (p37); 'Everyone sang' by Siegfried Sassoon, from Collected Poems, published by Penguin Books Ltd. (p43); extracts from Animal Farm by George Orwell, published by Penguin Books Ltd. (p46); extract from Holes by Louis Sacher, published by Bloomsbury (p48); extract from Cider with Rosie by Laurie Lee, published by Penguin Books Ltd. (p50); extract from My Family and Other Animals by Gerald Durrell, published by Penguin Books Ltd. (p51); extracts from 'Not My Best Side' by U.A. Fanthorpe, published by Peterloo Poets (pp56, 57); back cover blurb from World Party: The Rough Guide to the World's Best Festivals, published by Rough Guides (p60); extracts from Another Life by Derek Walcott, published by Jonathan Cape (pp62, 63); 'Midsummer, Tobago' by Derek Walcott, from Sea Grapes, published by Jonathan Cape (p64); extract from The Lonely Londoners by Sam Selvon, published by Penguin Books Ltd. (p69); extract from A Respectable Trade by Philippa Gregory, published by HarperCollins Publishers (p72); extract from Last Train from Kummersdorf by Leslie Wilson, published by Faber & Faber (p75); extract from Dreams of Anne Frank by I.B. Kops, published by Methuen Drama (pp82-3); leaflet from The Brooke donkey charity (p84); article from The Daily Telegraph by Melanie McDonagh, © The Telegraph Group 2009 (p88); article from The Big Issue by Michael Parker, all rights reserved (p90); 'Aunt Julia' by Norman MacCaig, from Collected Poems, published by Random House (p92).

The publishers would like to thank the following for permission to reproduce pictures in these pages.

Alamy (pp6, 25, 32, 45, 51, 58, 68, 70, 72); Bridgeman Art Library (pp56, 62, 74, 78); Getty Images (pp8, 37, 690; Imperial War Museum (p42); istockphoto (pp7, 12, 13, 14, 18, 23, 26, 30, 31, 39, 47, 50, 53, 60, 64, 76); Mary Evans Picture Library (p49); PA Photos (pp10, 36); Rex Features (pp11, 21, 33, 35, 46).

Contents

Chapter 1

AF2 Understand, describe, select or retrieve information, events or ideas from text, and use quotation and reference to texts   5

1 Summarise and synthesise information   6

2 Select and explore evidence from different texts   8

3 Make relevant points clearly identified with apt quotations   10

4 Understand how a line of argument is developed   12

Chapter 2

AF3 Deduce, infer or interpret information, events or ideas from texts   17

1 Make inferences from challenging texts   18

2 Interpret key points from different parts of texts   20

3 Consider the wider implications of themes, events and ideas in texts   22

4 Explore the connotations of words and images   24

5 Explore what can be inferred from the finer details of texts   26

Chapter 3

AF4 Identify and comment on the structure and organisation of texts   29

1 Comment on how successfully writers have opened their stories   30

2 Explore how writers structure a whole text   32

3 Recognise and discuss the effect of a range of structural features in a text   34

4 Comment on writers' use of narrative structure to shape meaning   36

5 Compare the organisation and development of a theme through a whole text   38

Chapter 4

AF5 Explain and comment on writers' use of language, including grammatical and literary features at word and sentence level   41

1 Identify and comment on emotive language   42

2 Explain and comment on authors' use of irony   44

3 Analyse how writers use different sentence structures and rhythms   46

4 Explore different kinds of dialogue in fiction   48

5 Compare how writers use descriptive language in different texts   50

Chapter 5   **AF6 Identify and comment on writers' purposes and viewpoints, and the overall effect of the text on the reader**   **55**

1 Use detailed evidence from a text to identify the writer's purpose (Part 1)   56

2 Use detailed evidence from a text to identify the writer's purpose (Part 2)   58

3 Give detailed evidence for your opinions at word, sentence and text levels   60

4 Explain writers' viewpoints using detailed textual evidence   62

5 Understand a text's effect on the reader and explain how the writer has created it   64

Chapter 6   **AF7 Relate texts to their social, cultural and historical traditions**   **67**

1 Recognise textual conventions   68

2 Recognise how textual conventions can be combined to create a new literary form   70

3 Discuss how ideas are treated differently in different times and places   72

4 Discuss how racism in texts is read differently in different times and places   74

5 Discuss how the same literary form is used differently in different times   76

Chapter 7   **Longer texts and reading activities**   **81**

1 I.B. Kops, from *Dreams of Anne Frank*   82

2 The Brooke donkey charity leaflet   84

3 Wilkie Collins, from *The Woman in White*   86

4 Melanie McDonagh, 'The death of handwriting impoverishes us'   88

5 Michael Parker, 'Final Chapter?'   90

6 Norman MacCaig, 'Aunt Julia'   92

Teacher Guide   **95**

AF2 Understand, describe, select or retrieve information, events or ideas from text, and use quotation and reference to text

This chapter is going to show you how to

- Summarise and synthesise information
- Select and explore evidence from different texts
- Make relevant points clearly identified with apt quotations
- Understand how a line of argument is developed.

What's it all about?

Using quotations to develop and support your ideas.

This lesson will
- help you to select relevant information from a text.

When you are reading a longer text you may need to pull out key information or reduce the text to its most important parts.

Getting you thinking

In pairs, imagine you are researching a holiday in Marrakesh. Read the travel brochure below.

Marrakesh and the Atlas Mountains

Six days from only £499

To visit Morocco is an intense and rewarding experience. A melting pot of European, Asian and African cultures, its blend of old and new will not fail to enchant you, whilst the sights, sounds and colours of this spectacular country will capture your heart and your imagination. From the romance of ochre-coloured Marrakesh, full of myths and mystery, to the splendid isolation of the Atlas mountains – it is an assault on the senses.

Day 1 You arrive at the airport to take the flight to Marrakesh. On arrival a coach will take you to the four-star Hotel Asni, for five nights' dinner, bed and breakfast.

Day 2 Marrakesh is a labyrinth of tiny alleyways, which team with street life like few other places in the world. With classical French colonial buildings and boulevards surrounded by almost medieval walls – it is so perfect it could be, and often is, a film set! This morning you have a sight-seeing tour during which you will see the Saadian tombs, one of the world's finest examples of Moorish architecture, whose classic archways are covered in gold-leaf and stucco work, and the El Badi Palace which, when built, was acclaimed as the world's most beautiful and famed for its 50 marble columns. You also visit the famous souks, or covered markets, where immensely skilled craftsmen create intricate leatherware, jewellery and furniture. At dusk you should visit Djemaa el Fna, a showcase for traditional Moroccan life. You will experience a fantastic spectacle of musicians, dancers, fortune-tellers and snake charmers in a kaleidoscope of colour.

- First, identify the key sections of the text.
- What in the description makes you want to visit Marrakesh? Summarise your ideas in one paragraph.

Now you try it

1 What picture of Morocco (outside of Marrakesh) is given in this article?

2 How does the writer use language to make a holiday there sound worthwhile?

3 Is any purely factual information given?

Development activity

In pairs, decide what aspects of the text about Egypt (below) make the market seem unattractive.

The colonial edifice of the train station marks one end of the market that is Aswan's bazaar. Through a neat undecorated Arabic archway the gauntlet begins:

'Come look in my shop. Nice things.'

'Just look, no hassle.' Says the man who has run out from his shop to tug at my arm.

'Hello, where are you from?'

'English? Lovely Jubbly! Asda price!'

'Just look, no hassle.'

'You want spices?'

'Look,' he brandishes a badly made embroidered blouse, 'lovely for your wife.' And when we ignore him and step round him, 'What? You not love your wife?'

'I pay you for looking. Come and look.'

'You want spices?' He steps in front of us and points at one of the spice stalls with neat pyramids of colourful spices arranged at the front. 'Look at that blue one, do you know what that is?' he insists, pointing out the vibrant indigo amongst the spice display.

By R. Bentley-Davies

- Record any words or phrases which make the market sound (a) unattractive (b) intriguing.
- What do you think is the overall purpose of this article?
- Imagine you are being asked about the market and whether you think it is worth visiting. Summarise the market's good and bad points in three sentences.

Check your progress

LEVEL 5	I can select relevant parts of information in a text
LEVEL 6	I can identify the most relevant parts of information in a text
LEVEL 7	I can discriminate between the relevance of parts of a text

This lesson will
- help you to make detailed comparisons between two poems.

These pages will show you how to make comparisons between two poems using apt quotations from the text.

Getting you thinking

Have a look at the first section of 'Preludes' by T.S. Eliot.

Preludes

I

The winter evening settles down
With smell of steaks in passageways.
Six o'clock.
The burnt-out ends of smoky days.
And now a gusty shower wraps
The grimy scraps
Of withered leaves about your feet
And newspapers from vacant lots;
The showers beat
On broken blinds and chimney-pots,
And at the corner of the street
A lonely cab-horse steams and stamps.

And then the lighting of the lamps.

In pairs, discuss the following questions:
- What does this poem seem to be about?
- What is the poem's setting?
- What sort of atmosphere or feeling is conveyed in the poem?

Remember to support your ideas with evidence from the text.

Which of the following comments do you agree (or disagree) with? Can you find any quotations to support your ideas?

A. It creates a depressing atmosphere.
B. The city seems very alive and jolly.
C. The poet uses the senses well.
D. You can tell it is set in another time.

Now you try it

In pairs, read the opening of this poem by Philip Larkin.

Friday Night at the Royal Station Hotel

Light spreads darkly downwards from the high
Clusters of lights over empty chairs
That face each other, coloured differently.
Through open doors, the dining-room declares
A larger loneliness of knives and glass
And silence laid like carpet. A porter reads
An unsold evening paper. Hours pass,
And all the salesmen have gone back to Leeds,
Leaving full ashtrays in the Conference Room.
In shoeless corridors, the lights burn.

1 Discuss with your partner what you think the poem is about.

2 Find three pieces of evidence that suggest loneliness in this poem. (For example, the word itself, an image, a detail, a weary rhythm or tone.)

3 Now compare the two poems:
   ◦ What effect does the time of day have in each poem?
   ◦ Which poem did you find the most effective in describing atmosphere and setting? Find evidence from the poem to support your view.

Development activity

Write up your comparison, using at least three paragraphs. Make sure you use at least one quotation to back up each point and explain its effect on the reader.

You could use a table like this to plan your ideas.

Lines that create a powerful feeling	What do these lines mean?
'And silence laid like carpet.'	The room is empty and silent. Saying silence is 'laid like carpet' makes it sound thick and dense.

Check your progress

LEVEL 5 I can read across several texts and pick out the most relevant points

LEVEL 6 I can pick out specific evidence from across a range of texts

LEVEL 7 I can analyse the effectiveness of different quotations

This lesson will
- help you to select a few words or a word as a quotation to prove your point.

A Level 6 reader can identify the central ideas in a text, and select short, apt quotations to prove their points.

Getting you thinking

Below is an extract from *The First Four Minutes*, the autobiography of Sir Roger Bannister, who was the first person to run a mile in under four minutes.

As we lined up for the start I glanced at the flag again. It fluttered more gently now, and the scene from **Shaw's *Saint Joan*** flashed through my mind, how she, at her desperate moment, waited for the wind to change. Yes, the wind was dropping slightly. This was the moment when I made my decision. The attempt was on.

There was complete silence on the ground… a false start… I felt angry that precious moments during the lull in the wind might be slipping by. The gun fired a second time... Brasher went into the lead and I slipped effortlessly behind him, feeling tremendously full of running. My legs seemed to meet no resistance at all, as if propelled by some unknown force.

We seemed to be going so slowly! Impatiently I shouted 'Faster!' But Brasher kept his head and did not change the pace. I went on worrying until I heard the first lap time, 57.5 seconds. In the excitement my knowledge of pace had deserted me. Brasher could have run the first quarter in 55 seconds without my realising it, because I felt so full of running, but I should have had to pay for it later. Instead, he had made success possible.

Glossary

Shaw's Saint Joan: a play by George Bernard Shaw about the life and death of St Joan of Arc

- In pairs, discuss how the writer has tried to make the race sound exciting. Use short quotations to support your answer.

Now you try it

In this next extract, Richard Branson explains how he started out in business.

My very first business enterprises, or moneymaking schemes, were not a success, but I learned from them. One Easter holiday, when I was about nine years old and home from prep school, I came up with a great plan. I would grow Christmas trees. Everyone wanted a Christmas tree, so it seemed logical to conclude that quite literally Christmas trees were a cash crop – and what's more, they just grew themselves. Pound signs danced in my eyes. I found out where to get seedlings and sent away for them. As soon as they arrived, I asked my best friend, Nik Powell, to help me plant some 400 seedlings in our field at home. We worked hard making holes with a gadget called a dibble and dropping in the seedlings, but like all boys who like to mess about on the farm, we also enjoyed ourselves. All we had to do was wait for the seedlings to turn into Christmas trees in eighteen months, sell them and count the money. Even at an early age I planned long term.

[…] Sadly, rabbits ate all the seedlings. We got some revenge. I'm sorry to say we had fun shooting the rabbits, which we sold for a shilling each to the local butcher. Overall, we did make a small profit on the original £5 investment and all our friends had rabbit pie. We all – except the rabbits – gained something.

How has the writer tried to make his first business idea sound exciting? Use quotations to support your answer and consider the following points:

- What words, phrases and metaphors does Richard Branson use to make his ideas sound exciting?
- What details does he give to help you imagine the work?
- What concluding point does he make?

Check your progress

LEVEL 5	I am able to select short, relevant and meaningful quotations
LEVEL 6	I can select short quotations and discuss their meaning in detail
LEVEL 7	I can use one-word quotations and analyse their meaning

4 Understand how a line of argument is developed

This lesson will

● help you to understand how a line of argument is developed.

A Level 6 reader can trace a line of argument in a text and support their ideas by using precise quotations and examining their impact.

Getting you thinking

In pairs, read this newspaper article and discuss the questions below:

First the snow, now the ice

Britain in the grip of harshest winter weather for 18 years

Britain faces a week of paralysis after the heaviest snow for at least 18 years shut 2,800 schools and bought chaos to the road, rail and bus networks.

Conditions were due to become even more treacherous last night as temperatures fell below freezing, turning the slush to ice.

Forecasters said that the blizzards would return to the South tomorrow, with sleet and snow continuing until at least the end of the week.

One in five workers took a 'snow day' yesterday. Supermarkets saw a rush from shoppers buying ready meals, soups and porridge amid fears that supply lines could be affected.

1 What is the writer's line of argument? How does he want the reader to feel about the situation?

2 Pick out two words you think are intended to alarm the reader. Explain your choices.

3 Try to write out your answers so that you have made a point, used a single-word quotation and explained its effect.

How does it work?

1 The line of argument suggests that this is the harshest winter for 18 years, citing the following evidence:

1 this is the heaviest snowfall in that period

2 there is transport chaos

3 ice is making conditions worse

4 more snow is forecast

5 one in five took a day off.

2 Here are two student responses to question 2. Which do you think is most successful at showing how a single word can reveal the writer's attitude?

Response A

One word that really shows the writer's attitude is 'treacherous'. The writer is making the point that the country is under threat and people face danger. 'Treacherous' sounds powerful and almost evil. We often describe people as 'treacherous' to suggest they mean us harm; here the word suggests the lethal condition of the roads and the danger they threaten.

Response B

'Conditions were due to become even more treacherous' is where the article shows the writer's attitude. He is most alarmed. This is because it sounds serious and dangerous.

Below is the opening of another newspaper article from the same day.

Snowbound Britain

Road, rail and airport bosses face anger as services grind to a halt

Large swathes of Britain came to a standstill yesterday in the grip of the worst snowstorms for 18 years. Despite five days of severe weather warnings, transport bosses still appeared to have been completely caught out as up to a foot of snow fell across the country, bringing rail, air and road networks to a halt.

Yesterday, they faced a growing public backlash as one in five workers was left stranded at home, at an estimated cost to the economy of £1.2 billion.

In London, all bus services were cancelled for the first time in living memory, as a network which had carried on running during the Blitz – and during much worse conditions in 1963 – proved unable to deal with six inches of snow. Cancelled Tube trains added to the chaos in the city.

[...] As hundreds of train services and flights were stopped and drivers faced treacherous conditions on ungritted roads, angry commuters demanded to know why the severe weather warnings had not been properly heeded.

Nigel Humphries, of the Association of British Drivers, said there could be no excuse for the failure of transport authorities to prepare for 'entirely predictable weather conditions'.

1 Read the newspaper article carefully and decide
   what the line of argument is.

2 What **individual word choices** best convey the writer's
   argument? Copy and complete the table below:

Short quotation from the text	Why have these particular words been used?	What does this tell us about the writer's attitude?
'services grind to a halt'		

Development activity

1 Who do you think the writer blames for the transport
   problems?

2 How is this different from the argument of the
   first article?

Remember

Use short quotations in
your answers and try to
discuss the effect of
individual words.

Level Booster

LEVEL 5

- I can select relevant parts of information in a text
- I can read across several texts and pick out the most relevant points
- I can select short, relevant and meaningful quotations
- I can make good and accurate points about a text and support them with my own opinion and a quotation

LEVEL 6

- I can identify the most relevant parts of information in a text
- I can pick out evidence from across a range of texts
- I can select short quotations and discuss their meaning in detail
- I can trace a line of argument

LEVEL 7

- I can discriminate between the relevance of parts of a text
- I can analyse the effectiveness of different quotations
- I can use one-word quotations and analyse their meaning
- I can explain how a line of argument has been developed

Chapter 2

AF3 Deduce, infer or interpret information, events or ideas from texts

This chapter is going to show you how to

- Make inferences from challenging texts
- Interpret key points from different parts of texts
- Consider the wider implications of themes, events and ideas in texts
- Explore the connotations of words and images
- Explore what can be inferred from the finer details of texts.

What's it all about?

Interpreting deeper levels of meaning in texts.

This lesson will
- help you to understand the deeper meanings of poems.

To make inferences from what you read means that you look beyond the obvious meaning.

For example, if you said to someone, 'Let's put it this way, she's no Lily Allen', this could **imply** that whoever you are talking about is not a good singer, not pretty, not feisty, not famous (any or all of these at once) – but it never states it. The reader or listener **infers** it.

Getting you thinking

Read the opening of this poem by Sophie Hannah – it states some things and implies others – and then answer the questions below.

Early Bird Blues

I am the early bird.
I have worn out my shoes
Simply because I heard
First come was first to choose.
One of my talents is avoiding queues.

I never ask how long
I shall be made to wait.
I have done nothing wrong.
I don't exaggerate.
To state the obvious, I'm never late.

Why has the queue not grown?
Nobody hears me speak.
I stand here all alone
Which makes me look unique
But even so, the worm avoids my beak...

Remember

Proverbs are short, well-known sayings which state a truth or piece of advice.

1 Explain how this poem takes a fresh look at the proverb *'The early bird catches the worm'*.

2 Look at the title of the poem. What do you know about the 'blues' and what can you infer about the poem from this?

How does it work?

Here is an example of a Level 6 response to the questions.
Notice how the student uses examples from the poem to
back up his **inferences**.

1 The poem takes a fresh look at the proverb, 'the early bird
catches the worm', by using irony. The proverb **implies** that by
being well prepared, success is guaranteed but the poem
suggests the exact opposite. In verse 1, the narrator states
'I heard first come was first to choose', but in the final stanza
it is evident that she is in the wrong queue, as she asks, 'why
has the queue not grown?' The stanza finishes with the
narrator standing 'all alone' and not having success, 'The worm
avoids my beak'.

2 The title of the poem implies that instead of a bird singing its
early dawn chorus happily, it has 'the blues'. This creates a
melancholy tone and supports the narrator's feelings of
sadness – as all her efforts to be well prepared have ended
in failure.

This response is clear and shows that the student is able
to 'identify different layers of meaning' which is
required at Level 6.

Glossary

Imply: what the writer or
speaker **hints** at but
doesn't say directly

Infer: what a reader or
listener **works out**

Development activity

1 What can you **infer** about the narrator in this poem?
She states she is a bird. Is she?

2 Explain how and why the poet adopts a persona (a bird).

Check your progress

LEVEL 5	I can understand the purpose of proverbs
LEVEL 6	I can make inferences about different parts of poems
LEVEL 7	I can compare two different poems using examples from each and explaining my choices

This lesson will
● help you to work out what is being implied at different stages of texts.

It is often necessary to interpret information from the different parts of a text. For example, if you are reading a newspaper article, you might learn the age of a fever victim at the beginning – then later that they are the youngest ever victim of that fever. The same could apply to a poem or a play.

Getting you thinking

Read the opening stanza of Sophie Hannah's poem *Symptoms*. What does the final line – when taken with the rest of the stanza – suggest about being in love?

> Although you have given me a stomach upset,
> Weak knees, a lurching heart, a fuzzy brain,
> A high-pitched laugh, a monumental phone bill,
> A feeling of unworthiness, sharp pain
> When you are somewhere else, a guilty conscience,
> A longing, and a dread of what's in store,
> A pulse rate for the Guinness Book of Records –
> Life now is better than it was before.

How does it work?

Here is an example of a Level 6 answer.

The stanza lists lots of negatives about being in love, 'stomach upset ... a dread of what's in store', but the final line, 'Life now is better than in was before', turns the whole poem around. The final line suggests in relation to the rest that though there can be many difficult experiences when you are in love, life is better for it. It suggests that all the negatives are worth it.

The student shows that she has thought about the different information we get in the final line of the poem, and has related it back to the rest of the poem.

Now you try it

In pairs, mark up a director's copy of this extract from *Romeo and Juliet*. Write in the margins what you want the actors to do – what gestures, expressions or actions they should perform as they speak.

> **ROMEO:** If I profane with my unworthiest hand
> This holy shrine, the gentle sin is this.
> My lips, two blushing pilgrims, ready stand
> To smooth that rough touch with a tender kiss.
>
> **JULIET:** Good pilgrim, you do wrong your hand too much,
> Which **mannerly devotion** shows in this.
> For saints have hands that pilgrims' hands do touch,
> And palm to palm is **holy palmers'** kiss.
>
> **ROMEO:** Have not saints lips, and holy palmers, too?
>
> **JULIET:** Ay, pilgrim, lips that they must use in prayer.
>
> **ROMEO:** O, then, dear saint, let lips do what hands do.
> They pray, grant thou, lest faith turn to despair.
>
> **JULIET:** Saints do not move, though grant for prayers' sake.
>
> **ROMEO:** Then move not, while my prayer's effect I take.
> *(They kiss).*

Glossary

mannerly devotion: polite and proper behaviour suitable to a holy place

holy palmers: Christian pilgrims (holding a palm leaf to show they had been to the Holy Land)

1 Life for Romeo and Juliet certainly seems better after line 14 than it was in line 1! Find evidence from the text to back this up.

2 Copy out the last word of each line. What rhyme pattern is made? Does it change at the end? If so, to what effect, coming at the moment before they kiss? (Try speaking the final couplet aloud with your partner.)

Development activity **APP**

Does Romeo and Juliet's relationship change in these 14 lines? What is suggested by Romeo referring to hands in line 1 but a kiss by line 4? What has happened to Juliet's resistance (in line 10) by the end of line 14?

Write up your answers.

Check your progress

LEVEL 5	I can annotate a text to show my understanding
LEVEL 6	I can extract examples from a text linked to a particular theme
LEVEL 7	I can develop an in-depth response based on my ideas about a text

3 Consider the wider implications of themes, events and ideas in texts

This lesson will

- get you to think about how and why a writer might choose to write about a theme.

When we read, we make deductions about what is happening – these deductions are often to do with ideas, themes, characters or events. We also need to think about why the writer chooses to write about these ideas or themes in the way he does.

Getting you thinking

In pairs, read this description of a boy in modern London.

> I didn't come to London straightaway. I may be homeless and unemployed but I'm not stupid. I'd read about London. I knew the streets down here weren't paved with gold. I knew there were hundreds of people – thousands, in fact – sleeping rough and begging for coppers. But that's just the point, see? In Bradford I stuck out like a sore thumb because there weren't many of us. The police down here have got used to seeing kids kipping in doorways, and mostly they leave you alone. In Bradford I was getting moved on every hour or so. I was getting no sleep at all, and practically no money. People up there haven't got used to beggars yet. They're embarrassed. They'll make large detours to avoid passing close to you, and if somebody does come within earshot and you ask for change, they look startled and hurry on by.

Remember

A theme is an idea that runs throughout a text.

- What do we find out about homelessness in
  a) Bradford and **b)** London?

- What can you deduce about the narrator's **character**?
  Write a paragraph giving at least three examples.

Now you try it

Read the second extract and answer the questions below in pairs.

> I strode out of the station with my backpack and bed-roll, and it felt like a new beginning. This was London, wasn't it? The centre, where it all happens. It's big, it's fast, and it's full of opportunities. Nobody knows you. Where you're from and what's gone before – that's your business. It's a clean sheet – you can invent your own past and call yourself anything you choose.

1 What positive ideas about London does it suggest?

2 What negative ideas about London were suggested in the first extract?

3 What does the move from Bradford to London mean for the boy?

4 What can you deduce about why he is glad to leave Bradford behind?

Development activity

Think about the two extracts you have read.

1 Overall, how does the writer make you feel about children sleeping on the streets and begging?

2 Why do you think he chose to write about homelessness in the first person?

Both extracts, while all too true to life, are taken from a novel, *Stone Cold* by Robert Swindells.

3 What do you think the book will be about? What do you think the main **themes** of the book will be?

Try and explain your answers in detail with evidence from the extracts.

Check your progress

LEVEL 5 I can understand how characters and themes develop in a novel

LEVEL 6 I can answer questions and provide evidence based on the texts I read

LEVEL 7 I can make inferences about what I think will happen in a text and give reasons for this

This lesson will
● help you to understand connotation and denotation.

When you read, you need to consider not only what words, images or phrases **mean** (their **denotation**), but what they might **imply or suggest** (their **connotation**). For example, the word 'red' literally means the colour red, but it also **connotes** passion, anger or romance – it is associated with all these things.

Getting you thinking

Remember

Denotation = what a word means literally

Connotation = what a word suggests or implies

Here is a description of a scene in a girls' school.

The January term started with a scene of sheer disaster. A muddy excavator was chewing its way across the netball-court, breakfasting on the tarmac with **sinuous** lunges and terrifying swings of its yellow dinosaur neck. One of the stone balls had been knocked off the gate-posts, and lay in crushed fragments, like a Malteser trodden on by a giant. The entrance to the science wing was blocked with a pile of **ochreous** clay, and curved glazed drainpipes were heaped like school dinners' macaroni.

The girls hung round in groups. One girl came back from the indoor toilets saying Miss Bowker was phoning the Council, and using words that Eliza Bottom had nearly been expelled for last term...

The next girl came back from the toilet saying Miss Bowker was nearly crying.

Which was definitely a lie, because here was Miss Bowker now, come out to address them in her best sheepskin coat. Though she was wearing fresh make-up, and her eyes were suspiciously bright, her famous chin was up. She was brief, and to the point. There was an underground leak in the central heating; till it was mended, they would be using the old Harvest Road boys' school. They would march across now, by forms, in good order, in charge of the prefects.

● In groups, discuss what kind of atmosphere is built up in this passage.
● Pick three images from the passage that help to build up this atmosphere. On one side of A3 paper, draw what you think each image literally describes (its **denotation**), and on the other, what it suggests or implies (its **connotations**).

Glossary

sinuous: supple or bending
ochreous: yellow or brown in colour

Now you try it

In this next extract, the girls are on their way to the new school.

Then the marching columns came to a miserable little hump-backed bridge over a solitary railway-line, empty and rusting. Beyond were the same kind of houses; but afflicted by some dreadful disease, of which the symptoms were a rash of small window-panes, flaking paint, overgrown funereal privet-hedges and sagging gates that would never shut again. And then it seemed to grow colder still, as the slum-clearances started, a great empty plain of broken brick, and the wind hit them full, sandpapering facts and sending grey berets cartwheeling into the wilderness.

Think about the way that imagery is used here – in particular, by **personification** – to create a strong mood or atmosphere.

Glossary

personification: giving a non-human object or thing human characteristics

1 What kind of mood is created by the following images?
   - 'a miserable little hump-backed bridge'
   - 'a solitary railway-line'
   - 'houses … afflicted by some dreadful disease'

2 How does the description of the weather add to the mood?

3 What does the word 'funereal' suggest?

Development activity

Having read extracts of this story, what atmosphere and expectations have been set up in the opening?

Use PEE (point, evidence, explanation) to write up your ideas, including your earlier responses.

How do you think the headmaster and pupils at the boys' school will be feeling?

Check your progress		
	LEVEL 5	I can work out how images create a mood or atmosphere
	LEVEL 6	I understand the difference between denotation and connotation
	LEVEL 7	I can work out how language is used for a particular purpose

Explore what can be inferred from the finer details of texts

This lesson will
● help you to read closely and comment in detail on your inferences.

It is important that you make **inferences** about what you read. It is also important to **comment in detail** on these inferences, explaining your deductions and interpretations with close reference to the text.

Getting you thinking

Read the extract from the beginning of a story called *Nothing to be Afraid of* by Jan Mark.

'Robin won't give you any trouble,' said Auntie Lynn. 'He's very quiet.'

Anthea knew how quiet Robin was. At present he was sitting under the table and, until Auntie Lynn mentioned his name, she had forgotten that he was there. Auntie Lynn put a carrier bag on the armchair.

'There's plenty of clothes, so you won't need to do any washing, and there's a spare pair of pyjamas in case – well, you know. In case...'

'Yes,' said Mum firmly …

Mum almost told Auntie Lynn to stop worrying and have a good time, which would have been a mistake because Auntie Lynn was going up North to a funeral.

Auntie Lynn was not really an Aunt, but she had once been at school with Anthea's mum … Robin was not anything much, except four years old, and he looked a lot younger; probably because nothing ever happened to him. Auntie Lynn kept no pets that might give Robin germs, and never bought him toys that had sharp corners to dent him or wheels that could be swallowed. He wore balaclava helmets and bobble hats in winter to protect his tender ears, and a knitted vest under his shirt in summer in case he overheated himself and caught a chill from his own sweat.

● What can you infer about 'Auntie' Lynn's treatment of her son?

How does it work?

Here is a strong Level 6 response.

> *From the beginning of the extract, I infer that Auntie Lynn is very protective of Robin. Near the beginning of the extract, Jan Mark lists the different things that Auntie Lynn has provided for Robin – 'plenty of clothes', 'a spare pair of pyjamas'. From 'just in case', I infer that Auntie Lynn means the four year old might wet the bed but doesn't want to say this aloud. Auntie Lynn is quite a worrier about her son, for example Anthea's mum had to tell her to 'stop worrying', suggesting perhaps that she doesn't normally leave Robin with other people.*
>
> *Further on in the extract, Jan Mark implies that Auntie Lynn is over-protective of Robin. It says how she won't have pets in case of 'germs' and also, how Robin is almost comically over-dressed, even in summer. This all suggests that Auntie Lynn is in danger of smothering her son with too much care.*

Now you try it

Read the extract again. This time, write a detailed response **explaining** what you **infer** about the character of Robin. Check with the example response for help.

Development activity

Read the next extract from the story and discuss in pairs what is implied about Robin.

> His face was as pale and flat as a saucer of milk, and his eyes floated in it like drops of cod-liver oil. This was not so surprising, as he was full to the back teeth with cod-liver oil; also with extract of malt, concentrated orange juice and calves-foot jelly. When you picked him up you expected him to squelch, like a hot-water bottle full of half-set custard.
>
> Anthea lifted the tablecloth and looked at him.
>
> 'Hello, Robin.'
>
> Robin stared at her with his flat eyes and went back to sucking his woolly doggy that had flat eyes also, of sewn-on felt, because glass ones might find their way into Robin's appendix and cause damage.

Check your progress

LEVEL 5	I can make inferences about a character's behaviour
LEVEL 6	I can write a detailed response about a character based on the inferences I have made
LEVEL 7	I can take part in a discussion about a text and use my ideas in a detailed piece of writing

Level Booster

LEVEL 5

- I can understand the purpose of different types of words
- I can annotate a text to show my understanding of ideas
- I can understand how a text can affect readers
- I can make inferences about different parts of a novel

LEVEL 6

- I can make inferences based on different parts of poems
- I can understand that extracts from different texts can be linked to a theme
- I can understand questions and give detailed answers
- I can understand literary terms, such as denotation and connotation

LEVEL 7

- I can compare ideas in detail with explanations
- I can develop an in-depth response based on my inferences
- I can understand the purpose of language and use PEE to back up my ideas
- I can discuss my ideas and apply what I have learned to a detailed piece of writing

Chapter 3

AF4 Identify and comment on the structure and organisation of texts

This chapter is going to show you how to

- Comment on how successfully writers have opened their stories
- Explore how writers structure a whole text
- Recognise and discuss the effect of a range of structural features in a text
- Comment on writers' use of narrative structure to shape meaning
- Compare the organisation and development of a theme through a whole text.

What's it all about?

How writers structure text to shape meaning and develop ideas.

1 Comment on how successfully writers have opened their stories

This lesson will
● help you to discuss whether a story opens well.

Recognising whether a writer has opened a story well, and knowing what makes one story opening better than another will help you to discuss texts.

Getting you thinking

Read these two story openings.

A

Prince Latarno slowly rose to his feet, casting one malignant glance at the prisoner before him.

'You have heard,' he said, 'what is alleged against you. Have you anything to say in your defence?'

B

Only kids believed City Cemetery was haunted. But that changed the Halloween night fourteen-year-old William Armbruster disappeared. His body was never found.

1 Identify the different ways these two stories start. Do the writers use any of these things?
● plot
● setting
● character
● genre
● dialogue
● narration
● conflict

2 How successful do you think these openings are?

How does it work?

Both writers hook their readers with their openings. The first writer makes clever use of **character**, **dialogue** and **conflict**. The second employs **setting**, **genre** and the beginnings of **plot**. Each opening makes us want to find out more.

Other writers might use techniques like **first or second person narration**, **short**, **long** and **minor sentences**, or **times** and **dates** to grab the reader's interest.

Now you try it

Writers know they need a **hook** to make readers want to read on. Are you hooked by these openings?

C

'How long has your husband been missing?' Detective Whittier asked.

Mrs Brenner had dark angry eyes. 'Since this morning at ten o'clock.'

D

The hunter found a human head propped up by the roots of the tree. It was an old head, little more than a skull, with grinning jaws and gaping eye sockets.

'I wonder how that got here,' he muttered half to himself.

E

It was an eighty-cow dairy, and the troop of milkers, regular and supernumerary, were all at work; for, though the time of the year was as yet but early April, the feed lay entirely in water-meadows, and the cows were 'in full pail'.

F

The overcast sky causes him to snap on the Firebird's headlights. Even before reaching the on-ramp he is travelling at 60 mph. Shoved between his legs is a cold can of Budweiser that stains the crotch of his tight tan slacks.

1 Imagine that you are an editor at a publishing house. You have been given these stories to assess. Which has the best opening?

Think about

- whether the **characters** and **settings** have been introduced well
- whether a **conflict** is established
- whether the readers are left with unanswered questions they want answered
- whether **dialogue** is used effectively.

2 Give each opening a mark out of 5 and explain why you have awarded this mark using the points above to guide you.

Development activity

Look at openings C and D with a partner. Discuss how each story's narrative viewpoint is likely to affect the way the story is written and structured. What difference might it make if the story is told from Detective Whittier's or Mrs Brenner's point of view?

Check your progress

LEVEL 5	I understand a sequence of events in a story and a beginning, middle and end
LEVEL 6	I can discuss whether a story opens well
LEVEL 7	I can comment on how successfully writers have opened stories

This lesson will
- help you to discuss the structure of a whole text in detail.

Being able to analyse the structure of an article and recognise the techniques that writers use to create an effective structure will help you to discuss texts in detail.

Getting you thinking

Read the article from *Cosmo Girl online* below. Discuss with a partner how the writer

- engages the reader's interest
- develops a clear theme
- makes her purpose for writing clear
- brings the article to a conclusion.

New York – home is where the heart is

Lately, I've been struggling with the definition of home. When you're traveling, the first thing people want to know, even before your name, is where you are from. It's a simple enough question, but my answer is pretty complicated. Is home where you grew up? (That would be Guam, USA.) Is it where you were born? (San Francisco) Where you keep all your stuff? (New York City) Where your parents live? (Guam and Rome) Where you declare residency for voting? (New Jersey) Where you last paid rent? (Paris)

I'm all over the map, as you can see. So when people ask me where I'm from, rather than launch into my life story, I tend to keep it simple. 'New York,' I say. It's where I feel the most at home. There's something magical about New York, especially during Christmastime. The city is alive with lights and possibility, and you always manage to stumble on something fascinating – incredibly talented street performers, crafts fairs, television show filmings. When I was going to college in New Jersey, I would always escape campus to come into the city. The energy on the streets would instantly invigorate me.

Thankfully, my travels have finally taken me back. I am writing this entry in a Starbucks in Union Square while sipping on a Gingerbread Latte and nibbling on a massive Rice Krispies treat – man, I missed them when I was in Europe! Outside, it's snowing, and the streets are lit up with twinkle lights. Even though I plan to continue traveling and exploring the world, I have to be honest – it's good to be home.

Now you try it

○ Here is another article from *Cosmo Girl online*.

Finding the Christmas Spirit

Holiday music is great, but when I am looking to get into the Christmas spirit, songs about riding sleighs and making snowmen just don't cut it for me. Instead, I turn to movies.

Christmas movies are normally exaggerated and silly, but I think that's what I love about them the most. In what other context can a grown man prance around in yellow tights, eating spaghetti drenched with syrup and singing carols everywhere he goes?

No matter what troubles I have, I will always laugh watching *A Christmas Story*.

And at some points, I can really relate to the Grinch in *How the Grinch Stole Christmas*. Sometimes, I'd rather dwell alone in my 'cave' than be among all the cheer. But I always appreciate when my own personal Cindy Lou Who comes to bring me holiday cheer.

Of course, there are always the classics like *Rudolph the Red Nosed Reindeer* and *The Muppet Christmas Carol*, which are perfect for watching with the family I haven't seen in ages.

What gets you into the holiday spirit?

How does the article use the following features or techniques to develop its theme, make its purpose clear, interest the reader and build to a conclusion:

○ topic sentences
○ reiteration of the central idea or theme
○ tone

○ rhetorical questions
○ first person voice
○ direct (second person) address to readers using pronouns like 'you'?

Development activity **APP**

Write a short article about your views on Christmas (or a seasonal holiday). Develop a tone – is it to be serious, full of wit, humorous?

Imagine your article is to be posted online. Make sure you exploit this!

Check your progress

LEVEL 5 I can recognise when a whole text is organised and structured

LEVEL 6 I can discuss in detail how a whole text is organised and structured

LEVEL 7 I can explore how writers structure a whole text

Recognise and discuss the effect of a range of structural features in a text

This lesson will

- help you to spot and discuss features that writers use to help them structure texts.

Recognising structural features will help you to discuss texts in detail.

Getting you thinking

Read this opening of the stage play, *Adrian Mole*. What structural features does the playwright use to give us a sense of Adrian's character?

Music: *The Mole Overture.*

At the end of the Overture, Adrian comes to the front of the stage. He talks directly to the audience.

ADRIAN

This is just my luck! I've come all the way from Leicester to hear a lecture about George Eliot only to be thwarted at the last minute because the American lecturer missed Concorde. What am I going to do now? I'm doing George Eliot for my English Literature project. I've written him loads of letters, but he hasn't replied to one. Still, with a bit of luck I might be able to mingle with a few intellectuals in the foyer.

He looks round at the audience.

There's loads here tonight. But I bet *they* don't live an ordinary life like me. No, they're lucky, they go home to book-lined studies and intellectual families.

Perhaps when my diary is discovered people will understand the torment of being a thirteen and three quarter year old intellectual. Until then I'll just have to put up with the charade that is my family life.

I bet Malcolm Muggeridge's family didn't carry on like mine did on New Year's Eve.

The lights go up to show the New Year's Eve party. Grandma and Mrs Lucas are sitting on the sofa. Pauline and Mr Lucas are dancing together. George is drinking from a can of lager. Adrian joins Nigel at centre stage. Everyone, including Adrian, is wearing a party hat.

Now you try it

What is the effect of **juxtaposing** Adrian's references to George Eliot, Concorde and intellectual life with the characters, props and actions of the New Year's party?

Glossary

juxtaposition: the placing of one thing next to another

Development activity APP

Now read this key episode from later in the play. Several students have been suspended from school for deliberately wearing the wrong socks.

PANDORA But, sir! What about our 'O' Levels...?

Scruton roars.

SCRUTON Quiet!

Everyone jumps.

NIGEL Can we wear our black socks with a red stripe. Sir?

SCRUTON No! Your socks must be entirely, absolutely, incontrovertibly dense, midnight, black!

Scruton exits.
Pandora starts to cry.

ADRIAN Now look what he's done. Don't cry, Pandora. Aren't you going to try to stop her, Nigel?

NIGEL No. She broke it off. She says I'm a philistine.

Nigel and the schoolgirl go off hand in hand.
Adrian pats Pandora's shoulder.

ADRIAN Don't cry. I've had a rejection letter from the BBC. Do you want to see it?

Pandora nods, she puts her head on Adrian's shoulder. He shows her the letter.
Music: 'Oh Pandora'.
Pandoru and Adrian walk together.
Voice over.

ADRIAN Pandora and I are in love! It is official! She told Claire Neilson who told Nigel who told me. I told Claire to tell Pandora that I return her love. I can overlook the fact that Pandora smokes five Benson and Hedges a day and has her own lighter. When you are in love, such things cease to matter!

Has Adrian's attitude to his real life changed? If so, how much?

Consider
- what **speeches** and **actions** show he either remains pompous OR has come to terms with his real life
- how **structural features** like music, voice over, dialogue, plot and juxtapositions combine to suggest any development in his character or situation

Write up your answer, drawing on evidence from both extracts.

This lesson will

● help you to discuss the way writers structure texts to help convey their meaning.

If you can make some detailed comment on how narrative structure shapes meaning, you are reading at Level 6. One of the most important ways a writer organises a text is the way he or she places it in time – for example, by the choice of tense or tenses.

Getting you thinking

Read this extract taken from *The Other Side of Truth* by Beverley Naidoo. In it, Sade and her brother Femi have arrived in London illegally from Nigeria. They are being questioned by police over an incident in a video shop.

'Do we know if they speak English?' asked Cool Gaze.
 'Oh, they speak English all right. I heard 'em!' declared Video Man. Cool Gaze now towered over them.
 'Look. If you've done nothing wrong, there's no need to be frightened.'

Papa has read the piece of paper and Joseph opens the gate. Men in khaki uniform and black berets surge into the yard. Papa is surrounded. Mama lets out a small cry.
 'Stay here!' she orders the children and rushes out of the sitting room to get to the yard. By the time she sprints down the steps, the police have hustled Papa out of the gates.
 'Where are you taking him?' Mama cries.
 Sade glimpses Papa's white shirt among the khaki as police push him into the back of their truck. No one answers Mama. The children run outside. When they reach Mama, the truck is already roaring down the road.

Sade had never felt so cold in all her life. Frozen inside and out. None of the people standing in front of her and Femi made any sense.

● How is time presented here? What structural devices does Naidoo use to help convey meaning?

How does it work?

The **past tense** is used for the main story, but **flashback** and the clever use of **present tense to show memories** that haunt her still (marked by **italics**) shape the meanings here.

Now you try it

Now look at the **mini saga**, *Like Mother, Like Son*.
How does the writer use time patterns and repetitions to
- suggest developments in plot
- create a link between past and present
- convey a moral?

Like Mother, Like Son

1955
Dear Mummy,
I hate this boarding school. Food awful, prefects bully me. Please take me home.
  Love, David

Dear David,
Nonsense! Chin up.
  Mother

1997
Dear David,
I hate this Home. Food awful, nurses treat me like a child. Fetch me immediately.
  Mother

Dear Mother,
Nonsense! Chin up.
  David

Development activity APP

1 What does the **juxtaposition** of present and past do in the extract from *The Other Side of Truth*?

2 What is the effect of the juxtaposition of the contrasts in the letters from *Like Mother, Like Son*?

Glossary

juxtaposition: the placing of one thing next to another

Check your progress

LEVEL 5	I can recognise when a text is organised and structured
LEVEL 6	I can discuss a few ways in which a text is organised and structured to shape meaning
LEVEL 7	I can comment on writers' use of narrative structure (including time) to shape meaning

This lesson will
- help you to compare the way ideas in two texts are put together.

The way a poet **organises the layout** and **structure** of a poem can help him or her develop a **theme**. The impact of such organisation can be seen if we compare two poems on the same theme.

Getting you thinking

Read this poem by Christina Rossetti about lost love. It is a **sonnet**, a 14-line poem with set rhythm and rhyme that often deals with 'deep' subjects such as love and death.

> REMEMBER me when I am gone away,
> Gone far away into the silent land;
> When you can no more hold me by the hand,
> Nor I half turn to go, yet turning stay.
> Remember me when no more day by day
> You tell me of our future that you plann'd:
> Only remember me; you understand
> It will be late to counsel then or pray.
> Yet if you should forget me for a while
> And afterwards remember, do not grieve:
> For if the darkness and corruption leave
> A vestige of the thoughts that once I had,
> Better by far you should forget and smile
> Than that you should remember and be sad.

In pairs, can you find examples of where the poet uses any of the techniques below?

- **rhyme:** the echoing of a sound, usually at the end of a line of poetry
- **rhyme scheme:** the pattern of rhyme in a poem
- **enjambment:** where the end of a line of poetry is not 'stopped' by punctuation – the sentence runs over into the next line
- **end-stopped line:** lines of poetry that are 'stopped' by punctuation
- **alliteration:** repetition of same or similar consonant (any letter that is not a vowel) sounds at the beginning of words
- **assonance:** repetition of vowel sounds
- **repetition:** repeating words, phrases, lines, often in a pattern (as in a chorus)

What do they add to the meaning and feeling of the poem?

Now you try it

In pairs, read this poem by Emily Dickinson, which describes the death of a loved one.

> You left me, sweet, two legacies,
> A legacy of love
> A Heavenly Father would content,
> Had He the offer of;
>
> You left me boundaries of pain
> **Capacious** as the sea,
> Between eternity and time,
> Your consciousness and me.

Glossary

capacious: vast, having lots of space inside

This is another poem about love, this time not told from the perspective of the person leaving or dying but from the person left behind.

- What words suggest this poem is about something big and important?
- What similarities or differences can you find in the form of the two poems? Compare them, using the table below. One comparison has been done for you. Find examples for each comparison and explain what the effect is of the writer's choices.

Rossetti's poem	Dickinson's poem
first person, personal account	
regular rhyme	
sonnet form	4-line stanzas (quatrains)
regular rhythm: iambic pentameter	
full rhymes at the end of lines	
theme of lost love	
powerful and intense feelings expressed	
medium-length lines	
alliteration	
enjambment	
repetition	

Check your progress

LEVEL 5 I can tell you about the form of a poem

LEVEL 6 I can understand why writers choose different forms for poems

LEVEL 7 I can compare the organisation and development of a theme through two poems

Level Booster

LEVEL 5

- I can recognise the genre of a text and understand reader expectations
- I can identify structural features in an opinion text
- I can understand the structure of a newspaper article
- I can discuss the effect of presentational devices in multi-modal texts
- I can understand why writers choose different forms for poems

LEVEL 6

- I can comment on how successfully writers have opened their stories
- I can explore how writers structure a whole text
- I can recognise and discuss the effect of a range of structural features in a text
- I can comment on writers' use of narrative structure (including time) to shape meaning and illustrate ideas
- I can compare the organisation and development of a theme through a whole text

LEVEL 7

- I can discuss whether writers have opened their stories in a successful way
- I can evaluate how well writers structure their texts
- I can evaluate a range of structural features and devices in a text
- I can explain how writers' decisions about narrative structure affect their meaning and ideas
- I can compare how well writers organise and develop a theme through a whole text

Chapter 4

AF5 Explain and comment on writers' use of language, including grammatical and literary features at word and sentence level

This chapter is going to show you how to

- Identify and comment on emotive language
- Explain and comment on authors' use of irony
- Analyse how authors use different sentence structures and rhythms
- Explore different kinds of dialogue in fiction
- Compare how writers use descriptive language in different texts.

What's it all about?

Explaining how writers choose words and construct sentences for maximum impact.

1 Identify and comment on emotive language

This lesson will
- help you to identify emotive language, what emotions it stirs up, and how effective it is.

Emotive language is language that deliberately stirs up the emotions of the reader or listener. It can be used in political speeches, leaflets or essays, and in adverts that encourage people to support campaigns for change – for example, to end child poverty or cruelty to animals. It is also used in poetry.

Top tips

Emotive language can stir up different emotions – such as anger, guilt, sympathy or hope.

Getting you thinking

Read the poem below, written by Wilfred Owen in reaction to the day-to-day killing in the First World War.

- What words and phrases do you find emotive?

Anthem for Doomed Youth

What **passing-bells** for these who die as cattle?
Only the monstrous anger of the guns.
Only the stuttering rifles' rapid rattle
Can patter out their hasty **orisons**.
No **mockeries** for them; no prayers nor bells,
Nor any voice of mourning save the choirs, –
The shrill, demented choirs of wailing shells;
And bugles calling for them from sad **shires**.

What candles may be held to speed them all?
Not in the hands of boys, but in their eyes
Shall shine the holy glimmers of goodbyes.
The **pallor** of girls' brows shall be their **pall**;
Their flowers the tenderness of patient minds,
And each slow dusk a drawing-down of blinds.

Glossary

passing-bells: funeral bells

orisons: prayers

mockeries: ceremonies which would seem meaningless in the circumstances

shires: counties

pallor: paleness

pall: funeral sheet

How does it work?

You don't need to understand every word of this poem to get a sense of its mood, and of the kind of emotions the poet wanted to arouse.

To comment on the poem, first look at the emotive phrases and consider what the poet is suggesting. For example:

Emotive word or phrase	What it suggests
'die as cattle'	This image suggests that the men are treated as if they are no more important than cattle, and have as little choice in their fate.
'monstrous anger of the guns'	This image makes the guns themselves sound angry, hinting at the aggression that has caused the war; 'monstrous' suggests something huge, ugly and immoral.

Now you try it

Discuss with a partner how Wilfred Owen's choice of words in the last six lines of the poem encourages the reader to feel sad about the war.

- Who might the girls be, and why is there 'pallor' on their 'brows'?
- Why are there no flowers for the soldiers, but simply 'patient minds'?
- What does the 'drawing-down of blinds' suggest? Who would be drawing the blinds down 'each slow dusk'?

Development activity

The following poem, by Siegfried Sassoon, is about the moment when the First World War ended. Write about the emotions it arouses in you as a reader, and how the poet's choice of words helps achieve this.

> Everyone suddenly burst out singing;
> And I was filled with such delight
> As prisoned birds must find in freedom,
> Winging wildly across the white
> Orchards and dark-green fields; on – on – and out of sight.
>
> Everyone's voice was suddenly lifted;
> And beauty came like the setting sun:
> My heart was shaken with tears; and horror
> Drifted away… O, but Everyone
> Was a bird; and the song was wordless; the singing will never be done.

Check your progress

LEVEL 5	I can identify emotive language
LEVEL 6	I can identify how emotive language arouses particular emotions
LEVEL 7	I can discuss and evaluate the effectiveness of emotive language

This lesson will

- help you to understand what irony is and how authors use it
- help you explain how effective writers' use of irony is.

There are two main kinds of irony. Situational irony is when something happens that seems especially unfair or inappropriate – for example, when someone drives over a cliff because they are trying to read a sign which says 'Danger: cliff'. The other kind, dealt with here, means saying one thing but really meaning something different.

Getting you thinking

In the extract below, Mark Twain (1835–1910) describes how he and his boyhood friends all wanted to work on a steamboat. This was not really glamorous or well-paid work.

Bearing that in mind, what phrases do you suspect are used ironically by this adult author looking back on his boyhood ambitions?

> By and by one of our boys went away. He was not heard of for a long time. At last he turned up as apprentice engineer or 'striker' on a steamboat. This thing shook the bottom out of all my Sunday-school teachings. That boy had been notoriously worldly, and I just the reverse; yet he was **exalted to this eminence**, and I left in obscurity and misery. There was nothing generous about this fellow in his greatness. He would always manage to have a rusty bolt to scrub while his boat tarried at our town, and he would sit on the inside guard and scrub it, where we could all see him and envy him and loathe him. And whenever his boat was laid up he would come home and **swell around** the town in his blackest and greasiest clothes, so that nobody could help remembering that he was a steamboatman;
>
> Mark Twain, *Old Times on the Mississippi*

Top tips

It is easier to give examples of irony than to explain it. It is more subtle than sarcasm, with which it is sometimes confused. The meaning is implied rather than plainly stated.

Glossary

exalted to this eminence: raised to this special position

swell around: go round showing off

How does it work?

In this passage, Twain is being ironic about his own boyhood ambitions.

The irony comes through the choice of words, such as the exaggerated phrase 'exalted to this eminence'. This suggests that the boy has been invited to sit next to God in heaven, or at least made Emperor of China.

Having a rusty bolt to scrub and wearing filthy clothes are hardly anything to show off about, but the young Twain thought that they were – so he is being ironic about himself, not about the steamboat boy.

Now you try it

Jonathan Swift (1667–1745) was a satirist – someone who criticises others using ridicule. He was from Ireland, then a very poor country ruled by Britain. His essay *A Modest Proposal* (1729) suggests what should be done with poor children in Ireland.

I have been assured by a very knowing American of my acquaintance in London, that a young healthy child, well nursed, is at a year old a most delicious, nourishing, and wholesome food, whether stewed, roasted, baked, or boiled; and I make no doubt that it will equally serve in a **fricassée** or a **ragout**.

I do therefore humbly offer it to public consideration that [the majority of poor Irish children] at a year old, be offered in sale to the persons of quality and fortune through the kingdom; always advising the mother to let them suck plentifully in the last month, so as to render them plump and fat for a good table.

Glossary

fricassée, ragout: types of meat stew

- Discuss with a partner how Swift uses irony in this extract.
- Explain to each other how you think the essay criticises the British government.

Development activity APP

Using the ideas from your discussion, write a short response to the following question:

Why do you think Swift uses irony to make his point about child poverty in Ireland?

Remember to bring in examples from the text and to explain their effect in your answer.

Check your progress

LEVEL 5 I can identify writers' use of irony

LEVEL 6 I can identify and explain authors' use of irony

LEVEL 7 I can identify, explain and evaluate authors' use of irony

This lesson will
- help you to understand how authors use different types of sentence structure.

Authors can use short, simple sentences or more complex ones. You need to be able to identify the different types, analyse their effect, and comment on their effectiveness, noticing how the variations develop a rhythm.

Getting you thinking

The following passage is from *Animal Farm*, by George Orwell. It is a novel that describes how animals rebel and take over the running of a farm from humans.

> In January there came bitterly hard weather. The earth was like iron, and nothing could be done in the fields. Many meetings were held in the big barn, and the pigs occupied themselves with planning out the work of the coming season. It had come to be accepted that the pigs, who were manifestly cleverer than the other animals, should decide all questions of farm policy, though their decisions had to be **ratified** by a majority vote. This arrangement would have worked well enough if it had not been for the disputes between Snowball and Napoleon.

- What do you notice about the different sentences used here?
- What kind of rhythm do these different sentences create?

Glossary

ratified: agreed

Now you try it

Read the continuation of the extract below.

> These two disagreed at every point where disagreement was possible. If one of them suggested sowing a bigger acreage with barley, the other was certain to demand a bigger acreage of oats, and if one of them said that such and such a field was just right for cabbages, the other would declare that it was useless for anything except roots. Each had his own following, and there were some violent debates. At the Meetings Snowball often won over the majority by his brilliant speeches, but Napoleon was better at canvassing support for himself in between times. He was especially successful with the sheep.

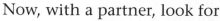

Now, with a partner, look for
- a short sentence (here, a **simple sentence**)
- **compound sentences** (simple statements joined by conjunctions like 'and' and 'but')
- **complex sentences** (with subordinate clauses).

Development activity

Here is a speech made by Queen Elizabeth I to her army in 1588, as they prepared to fight the Spanish Armada:

My loving people, **we** have been persuaded by some, that are careful of our safety, to take heed how we commit ourselves to armed multitudes, for fear of treachery; but I assure you, I do not desire to live to distrust my faithful and loving people.

Let tyrants fear; I have always so behaved myself that, under God, I have placed my chiefest strength and safeguard in the loyal hearts and good will of my subjects. And therefore I am come amongst you at this time, not as for my recreation or sport, but being resolved, in the midst and heat of the battle, to live or die amongst you all; to lay down, for my God, and for my kingdom, and for my people, my honour and my blood, even in the dust.

I know I have but the body of a weak and feeble woman; but I have the heart of a king, and of a king of England, too; and think foul scorn that Parma or Spain, or any prince of Europe, should dare to invade the borders of my realms.

Glossary

we: she means herself, 'the royal we'

1 In groups, read the speech aloud, with each person reading up to the next punctuation mark. Take care to express each clause in a way that makes its sense obvious.

2 Then discuss in your group how effective this is as a speech to encourage loyalty in an army. In your discussion, try to identify the sentence types: simple, compound and complex.

Check your progress

LEVEL 5	I can see how different types of sentence work grammatically
LEVEL 6	I can see how authors use different sentence types stylistically
LEVEL 7	I can evaluate authors' stylistic use of sentence types

This lesson will
- help you to understand how authors use dialogue effectively to reveal character and relationships between characters.

Dialogue brings a story to life and develops the plot. It can also reveal character. The *register* can be formal, as used by newsreaders, or informal, as used with friends. Characters may vary the register in which they speak. One challenge faced by authors is to make dialogue realistic yet dramatically effective. You need to be able to comment on how this is done.

Getting you thinking

In this extract from *Holes* by Louis Sachar, the boys are doing hard labour in an outdoor prison in a desert. Their punishment is to dig a hole each day.

> 'Well, how'd you like your first hole?' asked Squid.
> Stanley groaned, and the other boys laughed.
> 'Well, the first hole's the hardest,' said Stanley.
> 'No way,' said X-Ray. 'The second hole's a lot harder. You're hurting before you even get started. If you think you're sore now, just wait and see how you feel tomorrow morning, right?'
> 'That's right,' said Squid.
> 'Plus, the fun's gone,' said X-Ray.
> 'The fun?' asked Stanley.
> 'Don't lie to me,' said X-Ray. 'I bet you always wanted to dig a big hole, right? Am I right?'
> Stanley had never really thought about it before, but he knew better than to tell X-Ray he wasn't right.
> 'Every kid in the world wants to dig a great big hole,' said X-Ray. 'To China, right?'
> 'Right,' said Stanley.
> 'See what I mean,' said X-Ray. 'That's what I'm saying. But now the fun's gone. And you still got to do it again, and again, and again.'
> 'Camp Fun and Games,' said Stanley.

Remember

Authors may use dialect or slang in the dialogue of characters, especially when they are speaking informally. This can sometimes be difficult to understand.

Consider these questions:
- Who is the new boy?
- How do Squid and X-Ray get on?
- How formal or informal is their dialogue?
- What do X-Ray's comments reveal about his character?
- What can you tell about Stanley's character?

Now you try it

In the passage below, some Nottinghamshire miners, who are on strike, have just received their strike pay from their union. One man loses his money.

> They were drawing near to miserable Bulwell, when Ephraim, remembering his turn was coming to stand drinks, felt in his pocket for his beloved half-sovereign, his strike-pay. It was not there. Through all his pockets he went, his heart sinking like lead.
>
> 'Sam,' he said, 'I believe I'n lost that ha'ef a sovereign.'
>
> 'Tha's got it somewheer about thee,' said Chris.
>
> They made him take off his coat and waistcoat. Chris examined the coat, Sam the waistcoat, whilst Ephraim searched his trousers.
>
> 'Well,' said Chris, 'I'n foraged this coat, an' it's non theer.'
>
> 'An I'll back my life as th' on'y bit a metal on this wa'scoat is the buttons,' said Sam.
>
> 'An't it's non in my breeches,' said Ephraim. He took off his boots and his stockings. The half-sovereign was not there. He had not another coin in his possession.
>
> 'Well,' said Chris, 'we mun go back an' look for it.'
>
> Back they went, four serious-hearted colliers, and searched the field, but in vain.
>
> 'Well,' said Chris, 'we s'll ha'e ter share wi' thee, that's a'.'
>
> 'I'm willin',' said John Wharmby.
>
> 'An' me,' said Sam.
>
> 'Two bob each,' said Chris.
>
> Ephraim, who was in the depths of despair, shamefully accepted their six shillings.
>
> D.H. Lawrence, 'Strike-Pay'

Discuss in a group:
- what makes this dialogue sound informal
- how the writer uses dialect (local speech), and why he does so
- what the dialogue reveals about the characters and their relationships.

Development activity APP

Write a short comparative essay on both passages to help you sum up how dialogue in a story can (a) add dramatic interest and (b) reveal character and relationships.

Check your progress		
	LEVEL 5	I can see how authors use dialogue to reveal character
	LEVEL 6	I can see how authors use dialogue to reveal relationships
	LEVEL 7	I can evaluate authors' use of dialogue

49

This lesson will
● help you to make effective comparisons between the descriptive styles of different writers.

Writers use descriptive language in many ways – for example, in setting the scene in a novel or poem, travel writing, or biography. You need to be able to identify the author's purpose from the language used and the details included. You also need to be able to compare and evaluate different styles of description.

Getting you thinking

Read the two passages that follow, then select and write down any phrases that vividly bring to life the place described and the experience of the writer. Look especially for imagery – similes (using 'like' or 'as') and metaphors.

Top tips

When comparing authors, don't just write all you have to say about the first, then all you have to say about the second: try to keep comparing them all the way through what you write. The word 'Whereas' is useful here.

1 Laurie Lee, *Cider with Rosie*

I was set down from the carrier's cart at the age of three; and there with a sense of bewilderment and terror my life in the village began.

The June grass, amongst which I stood, was taller than I was, and I wept. I had never been so close to grass before. It towered above me and all around me, each blade tattooed with tiger-skins of sunlight. It was knife-edged, dark, and a wicked green, thick as a forest and alive with grasshoppers that chirped and chattered and leapt through the air like monkeys.

I was lost and didn't know where to move. A tropic heat oozed up from the ground, rank with sharp odours of roots and nettles. Snow-clouds of elder-blossom banked in the sky, showering upon me the fumes and flakes of their sweet and giddy suffocation. High overhead ran frenzied larks, screaming, as though the sky were tearing apart.

2 Gerald Durrell, *My Family and Other Animals*

This dolls-house garden was a magic land, a forest of flowers through which roamed creatures I had never seen before. Among the thick, silky petals of each rose-bloom lived tiny, crab-like spiders that scuttled sideways when disturbed. Their small, **translucent** bodies were coloured to match the flowers they inhabited: pink, ivory, wine-red, or buttery-yellow. On the rose-stems, encrusted with green flies, lady-birds moved like newly painted toys; lady-birds pale red with large black spots; lady-birds apple-red with brown spots; lady-birds orange with grey-and-black freckles. **Rotund** and amiable, they prowled and fed among the **anaemic** flocks of greenfly. Carpenter bees, like furry, electric-blue bears, zigzagged among the flowers, growling fatly and busily. Humming-bird hawk-moths, sleek and neat, whipped up and down the paths with a fussy efficiency, pausing occasionally on speed-misty wings to lower a long, slender **proboscis** into a bloom.

Glossary

translucent: semi-transparent

Rotund: round

anaemic: pale and lacking in vitality

proboscis: long mouth or sucking device

How does it work?

Both authors describe how the garden first seemed to them as children. They both use quite lavish language with a lot of adjectives and imagery, but there are important differences.

Laurie Lee	Gerald Durrell
Lee conveys a strong impression of a young child's experience. We see his height relative to the grass: 'It towered above me'. Lee suggests that the garden is exotic but threatening: 'each blade tattooed with tiger-skins of sunlight'. The double metaphor here suggests a dangerous jungle. The adjectives in 'knife-edged, dark, and a wicked green' also convey a sense of threat.	Durrell's garden is delightfully exotic but unthreatening: it's a 'dolls-house garden', 'a magic land'. Instead of talking about his own emotions, Durrell concentrates on the garden's inhabitants whose appearance and behaviour he describes in loving detail.
Lee favours metaphors, suggesting that for the three-year-old the garden actually is a jungle.	Durrell makes more use of similes: 'like furry, electric-blue bears'. These distance the author slightly from the thing described.

Now you try it

Now, on your own, make notes in answer to the
following questions:

- How do the two authors appeal to the senses?
- Which author uses viewpoint to create a certain
  amount of humour, and how?
- Which author makes animals seem almost human, and
  what effect does this have?
- Which author do you think was a professional
  naturalist, and how can you tell?

Development activity

In the following extracts, first Samuel Pepys (1633–1703), then
John Evelyn (1620–1706), describe the Great Fire of London.

In small groups, imagine you are a *London News* publishing
committee. You have to decide which account to publish.
Decide which one you think is more vivid and exciting, and why.

Pepys

[We] saw the fire grow; and, as it grew darker,
appeared more and more, and in corners and upon
steeples, and between churches and houses, as far as
we could see up the hill of the City, in a most horrid,
malicious, bloody flame, not like the fine flame of an
ordinary fire. ... We stayed till, it being darkish, we
saw the fire as only one entire arch of fire from this
to the other side the bridge, and in a bow up the hill
for an arch of above a mile long: it made me weep to
see it. The churches, houses, and all on fire and
flaming at once; and a horrid noise the flames made,
and the cracking of houses at their ruin.

Glossary

malicious: nasty,
deliberately taking pleasure
in destroying something

Evelyn

Oh the miserable and **calamitous** spectacle! Such as haply the world had not seen since the foundation of it, nor be outdone till **the universal conflagration thereof**. All the sky was of a fiery aspect, like the top of a burning oven, and the light seen above forty miles round about for many nights. God grant mine eyes may never behold the like, now seeing above ten thousand houses all in one flame; the noise and cracking and thunder, the hurry of people, the fall of towers, houses, and churches, was like an hideous storm, and the air all about so hot and inflamed that at last one was not able to approach it.

Glossary

calamitous: disastrous

the universal conflagration thereof: the end of the world

Check your progress

LEVEL 5	I can identify features of descriptive writing
LEVEL 6	I can compare different styles of descriptive writing
LEVEL 7	I can compare descriptive styles both in features and effectiveness

Level Booster

LEVEL 5

- I can identify and comment on metaphors and similes
- I understand how word choice affects tone and precise meaning
- I can comment on how authors use short sentences for dramatic effect, and how longer ones are structured
- I can appreciate and comment on formal and informal register in dialogue
- I can compare the effects of past and present tense in narrative

LEVEL 6

- I can identify and comment on the relative effectiveness of metaphors and similes in different types of writing
- I can compare the tone and exact meaning of word choices, and how they contribute to the overall mood of a text
- I can comment on how authors use short sentences for dramatic effect, and on how longer ones are structured using clauses
- I can appreciate how authors write effective naturalistic yet dramatic dialogue
- I can comment on the different uses of past and present tense narration and why authors use one or the other

LEVEL 7

- I can identify and comment on the relative effectiveness of metaphors, similes and personification, and on their appropriateness in a variety of different types of writing
- I can compare the tone and exact meaning of word choices, how they contribute to the overall mood of a text, and how they reflect an author's purpose
- I can comment on various ways in which authors use short sentences for dramatic effect, on how longer ones are structured using clauses, and how both can demonstrate the emotional state of characters in a story
- I can appreciate how authors write effective naturalistic yet dramatic dialogue, and how this compares with the use of reported speech
- I can comment on the different uses of past and present tense narration, how these affect the mood of a passage, why authors use one or the other, and how more complex tenses are sometimes used

Chapter 5

AF6 Identify and comment on writers' purposes and viewpoints, and the overall effect of the text on the reader

This chapter is going to show you how to

- Use detailed evidence from a text to identify the writer's purpose

- Give detailed evidence for your opinions at word, sentence and text levels

- Explain writers' viewpoints using detailed textual evidence

- Understand a text's effect on the reader and explain how the writer has created it.

What's it all about?

Explaining the effect of the text on the reader and how the writer achieves it.

Use detailed evidence from a text to identify the writer's purpose (Part 1)

This lesson will

● help you to analyse and respond to the range of purposes in a text.

Every text is produced for a reason. When we analyse a written text we need to act as detectives, looking for pieces of evidence that tell us why the author created it.

Getting you thinking

In U.A. Fanthorpe's poem, 'Not My Best Side', the dragon, the rescued virgin and the knight pictured in Uccello's painting *St George and the Dragon* speak their version of events. Here is verse II.

It's hard for a girl to be sure if
She wants to be rescued. I mean, I quite
Took to the dragon. It's nice to be
Liked, if you know what I mean. He was
So nicely physical, with his claws
And lovely green skin, and that sexy tail,
And the way he looked at me,
He made me feel he was all ready to
Eat me. And any girl enjoys that.
So when this boy turned up, wearing machinery,
On a really dangerous horse, to be honest
I didn't much fancy him. I mean,
What was he like underneath the hardware?
He might have acne, blackheads or even
Bad breath for all I could tell, but the dragon –
Well, you could see all his equipment
At a glance. Still, what could I do?
The dragon got himself beaten by the boy,
And a girl's got to think of her future.

● The legend usually casts the dragon as the villain, the virgin as a 'damsel in distress' and St George as the saviour.
● What evidence can you find that the poet wants us to rethink this?
● Does the girl's point of view surprise you?

Now you try it

St George speaks the third verse:

> I have diplomas in Dragon
> Management and Virgin Reclamation.
> My horse is the latest model, with
> Automatic transmission and built-in
> **Obsolescence**. My spear is custom-built,
> And my prototype armour
> Still on the secret list. You can't
> Do better than me at the moment.
> I'm qualified and equipped to the
> Eyebrow. So why be difficult?
> Don't you want to be killed and/or rescued
> In the most contemporary way? Don't
> You want to carry out the roles
> That **sociology** and myth have designed for you?
> Don't you realize that, by being choosy,
> You are endangering job prospects
> In the spear- and horse-building industries?
> What, in any case, does it matter what
> You want? You're in my way.

Glossary

Obsolescence: the ability to become out of date (in other words, to die)

sociology: the study of the development and organisation of human societies

St George is usually cast as a knightly hero from the Age of Chivalry – a Saint. He was supposed to be noble, both in the sense of being upper class and of being virtuous.

1 Find three quotations that suggest the poet wants us to rethink this.

2 Can you find evidence that *this* St George is (a) upper class (b) anything but noble?

3 What evidence suggests that this St George is, humorously, modern?

Explain to your partner why you have chosen each piece of evidence.

Development activity APP

Using your quotations and the explanations you gave your partner, write a paragraph or two, arguing that UA Fanthorpe's purpose is to question the stereotypes in the legend of St George.

Check your progress		
LEVEL 5	I can identify the main purpose of a text clearly
LEVEL 6	I can give detailed evidence for the purpose of a text
LEVEL 7	I can analyse a text to comment on its purpose

This lesson will
- help you to develop your interpretations of texts, supporting points with detailed evidence.

Every text has been produced for a reason. All texts – films, photographs, paintings, as well as writing – are put together with a purpose or purposes in mind. It can help to compare how a painting does this. Just as we examine a written text for details of word and sentence choices, we need to analyse the detail in visual texts to work out their purposes and meanings.

Getting you thinking

Remember

A text has usually been created for a number of different purposes.

Arnolfini Marriage, 1434

The picture was painted in 1434. No one really knows the story behind the painting but it gives us lots of interesting clues about the couple in the picture. Many people over the years have tried to work out why the painting was made. Now it's your turn!

1 With a partner, find these clues to the artist's **purpose** in producing this painting.

2 Discuss these questions with your partner:
- What event do you think the artist was commemorating?
- Where and why do you think the artist included himself in the painting?
- What clues tell you this?

Clue	Possible meaning
Arnolfini's hand is raised	He is greeting guests
A small dog	This **symbolises** faithfulness
Shoes have been taken off	This shows that something religious is happening
Candle burning	Represents the eye of God
Prayer beads	Show that the couple are religious
Oranges	These symbolise fertility
Chandelier	Shows that they are wealthy
St Margaret carved on the back of the chair	She is the patron saint of childbirth
Latin script above the mirror	It means 'Jan van Eyck was here 1434'
The couple are holding hands	What do you think this might mean?

Glossary

symbolises: stands for (like a white dove stands for peace)

How does it work?

Most art historians think that this picture was painted to show the wedding of this couple (symbolised by them holding hands and the shoes on the floor) and to wish them blessings (the candle), faithfulness (the dog) and children (picture of St Margaret and the oranges). The woman in the picture is probably not pregnant: that was the fashionable 'look'!

Now you try it

○ What was the artist trying to say about the event and the couple? How do you know?

With a partner, select five key features of this painting that suggest the answer to this question. You can use any of the 'clues' listed above or any other features you have noticed yourself.

For each one write a short paragraph explaining why you have chosen it.

Development activity

Use your notes to explain to the group what you think the artist's purpose was in creating this text.

○ Make sure that you use all five examples in your talk.

Check your progress		
	LEVEL 5	I can identify the main purpose of a text clearly
	LEVEL 6	I can give detailed evidence for the purpose of a text
	LEVEL 7	I can analyse a text to comment on its purpose

Give detailed evidence for your opinions at word, sentence and text levels

This lesson will
- help you to support your points with detailed evidence from the language the writer has used.

These pages will help you to apply your text-detective skills to a non-fiction text. You will analyse clues to the text's **purpose** and then think about how well that purpose is achieved.

Getting you thinking

This is the 'blurb' from *World Party: The Rough Guide to the World's Best Festivals*.

What is the **purpose** of this blurb? What evidence can you find for your answer?

You need to look for clues in the writer's choice of individual words and sentence structures, and think about the type of text this is.

> **The Rough Guide to the World's Best Festivals**
>
> Want to join the party?
>
> First hand accounts from the festival front line.
>
> World Party is the complete guide to the world's most spectacular festivals and celebrations, from Pushkar's amazing camel fair to the carnival in Rio.
>
> Explore every angle of over 200 events, from all over the world.
>
> Choose your festival by date, theme or country – or by chance – and plan as much, or as little, as you like.
>
> Read about the history and culture of each event, with expert insights to enrich your experience.
>
> Rely on Rough Guides' pick of the best places to stay, eat, drink and party with other festivalgoers.

1 Find examples of
- words that make this book sound like it has been written by knowledgeable people
- words or short phrases that make the book sound **comprehensive**
- words or short phrases that make the information in the book seem trustworthy.

Glossary

comprehensive: telling you everything you need to know

Now you try it

Now think about how the writer has structured the **sentences** to achieve their purpose.

1 Find these imperative verbs in the text: 'Explore', 'Choose', 'Read', 'Rely'.
  ○ Where do they come in their sentences?
  ○ How do they suggest that the writer is reliable and able to take charge of their holiday?

2 Choose one imperative and explain to your partner why it has been used.

3 What **clues** tell you what kind of person the blurb is aimed at?

Work with a partner to fill in a table like this:

Attribute of audience	Textual clue	Reason why they would read this book
Adventurous	'festival front line' implies danger and unexplored territory	To plan new challenges or to make them feel like they could go anywhere in the world.
Like to have information from 'insiders'		

Development activity APP

So, text-detectives, you have all your clues. Now use the information you have gathered to answer this question: **Does this text achieve its purpose?**

Make sure you have
○ an introductory paragraph in which you say what the purpose of the text is
○ at least three paragraphs making different points
○ a conclusion in which you give your answer to the question.

Re-read your work or swap with a partner. Does the answer:
○ use clues to work out the **purpose** of the text? (Level 6)
○ give precise evidence at **word** and **sentence levels** for their points (Level 6)
○ use clues from across the **whole text**? (Level 6)
○ explain why the text is **effective** at achieving its purpose for the target audience? (Level 7)?

Check your progress

LEVEL 5 I can identify the main purpose of a text clearly

LEVEL 6 I can give evidence for the purpose of a text at word, sentence and text level

LEVEL 7 I can comment on a writer's purposes analytically

4 Explain writers' viewpoints using detailed textual evidence

This lesson will
● help you to develop your skills in understanding and explaining the viewpoint a writer is using.

These pages will help you to develop your skills in understanding and explaining the viewpoint of a writer.

Getting you thinking

Here is the opening of a poem by Derek Walcott called 'Noon'.

> Noon,
>   and its sacred water sprinkles.
> A schoolgirl in blue and white uniform,
> her golden plaits a simple **coronet**
> out of **Angelico**, a fine sweat on her forehead,
> hair where the twilight singed and signed its **epoch**.

1 With a partner, make a list of the things we are told about the girl.

2 Next to each one write what you think the poet wants us to deduce from this information.

For example, you could start:

She looks like a character from a religious painting

She is being shown as like an angel.

Top tips

Do you always accept what people tell you without asking them to give you a reason? When we talk about texts we can't expect people to agree with our ideas without explaining our reasons.

Glossary

coronet: a small crown

Angelico: an artist who painted religious subjects such as angels

epoch: an important period in someone's life

How does it work?

This poem is written in the *third person*.

The narrator of the poem has described the girl to us as if he is watching her. He gives us a lot of information about what he thinks of her. Details like 'a simple coronet' and the 'fine' sweat on her forehead suggest the poem is narrated from the **viewpoint** of someone who loves or admires her.

Now you try it

Now read the next part of the poem. Here the poet explores the feelings of a young man towards the girl.

1 With a partner, write down two things that we learn about this young man's feelings. Which words tell you how he feels?

2 Do we understand more about his feelings or the schoolgirl's? Write a paragraph explaining your answer to this question. Remember to use examples from the text.

> And a young man going home.
> They move away from each other.
> They are moving towards each other.
> His head roars with hunger and poems.
> His hand is trembling to recite her name.

Development activity APP

Now read the whole poem:

1 With a partner, read the poem aloud. One of you should read the lines that focus on the girl and the other those that give us the viewpoint of the boy.

2 Now answer the following questions on your own. Write at least one paragraph for each, fully explaining your ideas.

a Choose one line you decided described the girl. Which words and phrases told you this?

> Noon,
>   and its sacred water sprinkles.
> A schoolgirl in blue and white uniform,
> her golden plaits a simple coronet
> out of Angelico, a fine sweat on her forehead,
> hair where the twilight singed and signed its epoch.
> And a young man going home.
> They move away from each other.
> They are moving towards each other.
> His head roars with hunger and poems.
> His hand is trembling to recite her name.
> She clutches her books, she is laughing,
> her uniformed companions laughing.
> She laughs till she is near tears.

b Choose one line you decided was told from the boy's viewpoint. Which words and phrases told you this?

c Were there any lines that were neither restricted to the girl nor gave the boy's viewpoint? Whose view were we seeing during these lines? Why?

3 Explain the overall **viewpoint** of the writer. How does he feel about the two characters in the poem? (Remember that the viewpoint can change during the poem.)

Remember to use evidence and to explain why you chose it.

Check your progress

LEVEL 5	I can clearly identify the writer's viewpoint and explain my ideas
LEVEL 6	I can explain the writer's viewpoint using detailed reference to the text
LEVEL 7	I can comment analytically on the way a writer establishes viewpoint in a text

This lesson will
● help you to analyse and respond to the effect the writer has created.

All texts have an effect on you as a reader. For example, they can make you like or hate a person or place being described. These effects are created through the writer's choice of imagery, words, punctuation, paragraphs or lines and stanzas.

Getting you thinking

Read this poem by Derek Walcott.

> **Midsummer, Tobago**
>
> Broad sun-stoned beaches.
>
> White heat.
> A green river.
>
> A bridge,
> scorched yellow palms
>
> from the summer-sleeping house
> drowsing through August.
>
> Days I have held,
> days I have lost,
>
> days that outgrow, like daughters,
> my **harbouring** arms.

The writer uses images to build up a picture of the place. He doesn't need to use many words because he's chosen them so carefully.

Glossary

harbouring: protecting, giving safety

● Look at the first seven lines of the poem. With a partner, choose pictures from the internet to illustrate each image in these lines.

Make a collage of the images in the poem, annotating each one with words or phrases from the poem to build up the picture Derek Walcott creates in our minds.

What do these images tell you about the place he is describing?

Now you try it

Copy out and annotate these two-line stanzas to show the effects Walcott creates through his use of language.

One has been done for you below as an example. Try to think about the following features:

- punctuation choices (how do they change the way you read the poem?)
- length of lines
- length of words
- sounds the poet has chosen
- carefully chosen adjectives and use of colour
- alliteration.

> A bridge,
> scorched yellow palms

> from the summer-sleeping house
> drowsing through August

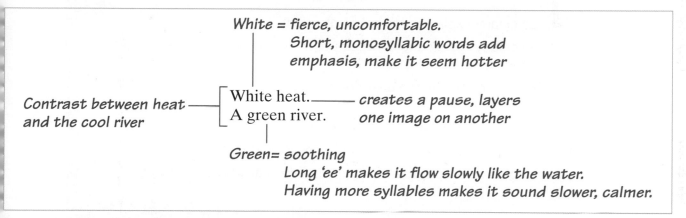

White = fierce, uncomfortable.
    Short, monosyllabic words add emphasis, make it seem hotter

Contrast between heat and the cool river —— White heat. —— *creates a pause, layers one image on another*
A green river.

Green= soothing
    Long 'ee' makes it flow slowly like the water.
    Having more syllables makes it sound slower, calmer.

Development activity APP

1 How does Derek Walcott make the reader feel about midsummer in Tobago in the first seven lines?

Plan your answer by considering:
- the effect of the poem on the reader – how it makes them feel
- the way he uses words and phrases
- the way he uses punctuation
- how effective you think these lines are.

For each bullet point make brief notes on what you would say and what evidence you would use to support your points.

2 Now use all your notes and examples to answer these questions: What effect has the poem had on you as a reader? How was this effect achieved?

Check your progress

LEVEL 5	I can explain what effect a text has on the reader
LEVEL 6	I can identify the effect of a text on the reader and say how it has been created
LEVEL 7	I can start to explain how a writer uses techniques and devices to achieve an effect

Level Booster

LEVEL 5

- I can identify what the writer is trying to achieve (the writer's purpose)
- I can identify the writer's viewpoint
- I can identify the effect a text has on the reader
- I can explain my ideas

LEVEL 6

- I can clearly explain the purpose of a text
- I can clearly explain the viewpoint of the writer or persona in more complex texts
- I can clearly identify the effect on the reader and say how that effect has been created
- I can give detailed evidence for my opinions at word level
- I can give detailed evidence for my opinions at sentence level
- I can give detailed evidence for my opinions at whole text level

LEVEL 7

- I can analyse a text to explain the writer's purpose
- I can evaluate how the writer's viewpoint develops across a whole text
- I can explain how the writer has used language to achieve the effect they intended

Chapter 6

AF7 Relate texts to their social, cultural and historical traditions

This chapter is going to show you how to

- Recognise textual conventions
- Recognise how textual conventions can be combined to create a new literary form
- Discuss how ideas are treated differently in different times and places
- Discuss how racism in texts is read differently in different times and places
- Discuss how the same literary form is used differently in different times.

What's it all about?

When we read, we are not just reading texts, we are reading the society and traditions they come from. This chapter will help you read the genres, times, places and cultures behind the texts.

This lesson will
- help you explore some of the conventions of travel writing.

Each form of writing has its own rules – called **conventions**. One of the conventions of travel writing is an eyewitness account – often by an outsider – of something strange or new. For it to work, the reader must be interested in the place, or in the original and unfamiliar way the writer sees it.

Getting you thinking

What is 'interesting' or unusual in this narrative? Is it the thing described? Or the unusual way it is seen? Or both?

It was about the beginning of the spring 1757 when I arrived in England, and I was near twelve years of age at that time. I was very much struck with the buildings and the pavement of the streets in Falmouth; and, indeed, any object I saw filled me with new surprise. One morning, when I got upon deck, I saw it covered all over with the snow that fell over-night: as I had never seen any thing of the kind before, I thought it was salt; so I immediately ran down to the mate, and desired him, as well as I could, to come and see how somebody in the night had thrown salt all over the deck. He, knowing what it was, desired me to bring some of it down to him: accordingly I took up a handful of it, which I found very cold indeed; and when I brought it to him he desired me to taste it. I did so, and I was surprised beyond measure.

Olaudah Equiano, *The Interesting Narrative*

How does it work?

White Europeans might find this African slave's first **experience** of snow more 'interesting' than **what** he sees. But fellow first-time Africans in Europe might share his fascination with snow, Western buildings and pavements. Good travel writing turns its readers into 'outsiders' – either to the thing described, or the view taken, or both.

Now you try it **APP**

The following extract gives an immigrant view of London in 1956. The narrator tells the story of the 'Windrush' generation newly arrived from the West Indies.

Many nights he went there before he knew how to move around the city, and see them fellows and girls waiting, looking at they wristwatch, watching people come up the escalator from the tube. You could tell that they waiting for somebody, the way how they getting on. Leaning up there, reading the *Evening News*, or smoking a cigarette, or walking around the circle looking at clothes in the glasscase, and every time people coming up the escalator, they watching to see, and if the person not there, they relaxing to wait until the next tube come. All these people there, standing up waiting for somebody. And then you would see a sharp piece of skin come up the escalator, in a sharp coat, and she give the ticket collector she ticket and look around, and same time the feller who waiting throw away his cigarette and you could see a happy look in his face, and the girl come and hold his arm and laugh, and he look at his wristwatch. Then the two of them walk up the steps and gone to the Circus, gone somewhere, to the theatre, or the cinema, or just to walk around and watch the big life in the Circus.

Sam Selvon, *The Lonely Londoners*

- In pairs, decide where the narrator is and what he is seeing. Is it as strange as it sounds?

- Do you think this extract is
  a an eyewitness account of a place or situation which is **unfamiliar or strange** to you
  b an unusual account of a place or situation you **do recognise**
  c both?

Remember

A writer chooses a form of writing first.

This form will have certain conventions.

The writer works within these conventions, but in his or her own way.

Check your progress

LEVEL 5	I can give some explanation of how non-fiction meanings can change through time
LEVEL 6	I can discuss in detail how non-fiction meanings can change through time
LEVEL 7	I can analyse how non-fiction meanings can be interpreted differently in different times

This lesson will

- help you tell the difference between different types of literary text
- help you understand the different conventions of particular texts.

Different texts have different **conventions**. These conventions can be about a text's language, structure or ideas, or a text's appearance or presentation. A major part of a text's meaning depends on its form – is it fiction or not, and if so, what kind?

Glossary

mantle: a loose wrap or cloak

courtesy: politeness

a nine hundred years old name: he's from an ancient aristocratic family

Getting you thinking

Look at this extract. An Italian Duke is showing a visitor around his private art gallery. He is wealthy and powerful – and evidently above the law. He is used to getting his own way, especially with his wives.

All of this is revealed by the Duke's own words to his guest about this painting of his 'last' wife by an artist called Frà Pandolf.

Ferrara
That's my last Duchess painted on the wall,
Looking as if she were alive;
　　　　　　[…] Sir, 'twas not
Her husband's presence only, called that spot
Of joy into the Duchess' cheek: perhaps
Frà Pandolf chanced to say 'Her **mantle** laps
Over my Lady's wrist too much,' or 'Paint
Must never hope to reproduce the faint
Half-flush that dies along her throat;' such stuff
Was **courtesy**, she thought, and cause enough
For calling up that spot of joy. She had
A heart … how shall I say? … too soon made glad,
Too easily impressed; she liked whate'er
She looked on, and her looks went everywhere.
　　　[…] She thanked men, — good; but thanked
Somehow … I know not how … as if she ranked
My gift of a **nine hundred years old name**
With anybody's gift.
　　　　[…] This grew; I gave commands;
Then all smiles stopped together. There she stands
As if alive. Will't please you rise? We'll meet
The company below, then.

- Do you think this is from a newspaper, poem, history book, novel, advertisement, play, travel book or something else?

How does it work?

This text has several **conventions** we expect of literature.

- It is written in **verse**.
- A person or **character** (Ferrara), who doesn't seem to be the writer, is speaking to us and we are being told a **story**.

History books or news have other conventions: for example, a less personal tone and a greater use of factual information. They would tell the same story in different ways.

Now you try it

But what **form** of literature is it?

1 Can you find any evidence that makes you think it is
- **a play** (Does it have a character? Someone who seems to be speaking to someone else? Is it set out like a play?)
- **a poem** (Does it use lines of verse or sound effects like rhymes?)
- **a story** (Does it use a 'made-up' character or tell about events that happened in the past? Does it have a narrator?)

2 If there **is** a story, what exactly happens? List the events – including the Duke's account of his wife's behaviour – in the order he reports them to his listener.

Start:

1. *He says she liked the attention of other men (it says 'twas not / Her husband's presence only, called that spot / Of joy into the Duchess' cheek').*

3 What do you think (or **imagine**) Ferrara has done to his 'last' Duchess?

Development activity

So, is this a story, play or poem? In fact, 'My Last Duchess' is all three – and none of them – at the same time! It is a **new form** called a **dramatic monologue**, developed by the Victorian poet Robert Browning.

You now know the ingredients of a **dramatic monologue**. But there is a final check: what do the words **dramatic** and **monologue** mean?

Write a paragraph, using examples from the poem to explain
- how **dramatic monologue** works
- what **conventions** it includes.

Check your progress

LEVEL 5	I can identify a dramatic monologue
LEVEL 6	I can identify a dramatic monologue and explore some of its features
LEVEL 7	I can analyse a dramatic monologue and explore its development as a literary form

This lesson will

● help you relate ideas in texts to the changing attitudes of our own society.

The way we read texts is influenced by our time and place of reading, and the values of our own society.

Getting you thinking

In the following extract, an African slave boy is about to die.

> Sarah straightened up, her face full of suppressed anger. 'You can make a big parade of your feelings over this,' she snapped. '…You can attend the funeral, you can hire a hearse. It is throwing bad money after good. The child is dying, and you knew when you started this that at least two or three would die during the first year. It is natural wastage. It is the natural loss of **stock**. If we have to go into mourning every time a slave dies we might as well grieve for a broken barrel of sugar.'
>
> 'He is a child,' Frances cried passionately. 'A little boy…'
>
> 'He is our Trade,' Sarah said. 'And if we cannot make this Trade pay then we are on the way to ruin. Wear black crepe if you like, Sister. But get those slaves trained and ready for sale.'
>
> Philippa Gregory, *A Respectable Trade*

● Whose side are you on, Frances' or Sarah's?

Glossary

stock: livestock, such as cattle or sheep

How does it work?

In this extract, modern readers will almost certainly side with Frances. A human child is dying. *We* are unlikely to read this tragedy as 'a natural loss of stock' or a 'broken barrel of sugar'.

But in the 1780s Bristol in which this story is set, many – including those who were kind and thoughtful in other ways – might have sided with Sarah. That society valued the (African) Trade for its slaves and the West Indian sugar, coffee, tobacco and rum it produced. With the exception of the growing anti-slave movement, this society did not value the human life of those slaves. Or only – and highly – as livestock valued at £50 per head.

Modern readers will read this extract from a completely different social context, one appalled by the slave trade, not one profiting from it.

Now you try it

1 In pairs, discuss the following:
   - Can you remember anything you wore last weekend?
   - Were you or was the person who bought your clothes pleased with the 'bargain' price? Or the 'label'?
   - Are you pleased with the quality, fit or style?
   - Do you know where – or how – they were made?

2 In pairs, imagine it is 2050. Imagine that this society makes it
   a illegal to pay Third World workers less than 90% of the value of their work and of the materials
   b illegal to buy or sell animal products, like leather or furs, as human clothing.

Now read the following advertisements from our own time:

Autumn collection now in store!

Subscribe to Cool Fashions Newsletter and receive the latest fashion news and fantastic offers. The brightest fabrics from Asia and Africa at a fraction of the price. And as a thank you, we will give you a welcome coupon of **20%** to use on your next purchase.

Winter Sale

Absolutely All SALE Items Half Price or Even Less

Leather.co.uk – shop online for the latest leather fashion. Heat-retaining but great-looking leather garments and snug-as-a-fox furs that fit like your own skin. Keep warm – and stay minky cool!

- How would your society in 2050 view these 'old' adverts?
- Discuss in role, as if you have just come across these adverts from 2009.

Development activity

Then, individually, write up your thoughts on
- why attitudes to texts change over time
- whether texts from previous times should still be read today, even if they show values different from our own.

Remember

Just as we 'read' the slave trade context differently from people in the 1780s, a future society might read **our** shopping habits differently.

Check your progress

LEVEL 5	I can give some explanation of how texts are read differently in different times
LEVEL 6	I can explore in some detail how texts are read differently in different times
LEVEL 7	I can analyse how texts are read differently in different times

73

4 Discuss how racism in texts is read differently in different times and places

This lesson will
- help you relate texts to changing attitudes about race and ethnicity.

Texts reflect the time and place in which they were written. The way we read these texts is also influenced by our time and place of reading.

Getting you thinking

Look at this episode from *Huckleberry Finn* by Mark Twain. Huck and his friend Tom Sawyer are caught mid-mischief by Jim, a black slave. But Jim can't see them. Huck is telling the story and the writing is very funny. But does it mock and stereotype African-American people and their culture?

'Who dah?'

He (Jim) listened some more; then he come tiptoeing down and stood right between us; we could a touched him, nearly … So he set down on the ground betwixt me and Tom. He leaned his back up against a tree, and stretched his legs out till one of them most touched one of mine. My nose begun to itch.

… Just then Jim begun to breathe heavy; next he begun to snore – and then I was pretty soon comfortable again.

… I was in a sweat to get away; but nothing would do Tom but he must crawl to where Jim was, on his hands and knees, and play something on him. I waited, and it seemed a good while, everything was so still and lonesome.

… Tom said he slipped Jim's hat off of his head and hung it on a limb right over him, and Jim stirred a little, but he didn't wake. Afterwards Jim said the witches be-witched him and put him in a trance, and rode him all over the State, and then set him under the trees again, and hung his hat on a limb to show who done it. And next time Jim told it he said they rode him down to New Orleans; and, after that, every time he told it he spread it more and more, till by and by he said they rode him all over the world, and tired him most to death, and his back was all over saddle-boils. Jim was monstrous proud about it, and he got so he wouldn't hardly notice the other [slaves … Slaves] is always talking about witches in the dark by the kitchen fire; but whenever one was talking and letting on to know all about such things, Jim would happen in and say, 'Hm! What you know 'bout witches?'

Now you try it APP

Look at this description (from a novel published in 2003) of boys tormenting an old Jewish man in Nazi Germany.

…an old Jew came along with an armful of books, he had a yellow star on, so we knew what he was. And we'd had a lesson in school about Jews, that day. So we started to yell at him. There were people standing there who could have told us to stop, but they didn't and Emil slapped his behind. The Jew just stood still and shivered, he didn't move. He dropped all his books and Emil kicked them into a puddle …

The teacher had told us Jews were bad, he said they had to be chased out of Germany, but – that man didn't look like the pictures in our schoolbooks, with those hook noses and blue chins … He was just an old man with white hair. And it felt wrong when Emil slapped his behind. Kids shouldn't slap old men.

… I felt ashamed. My mates were laughing at the Jew because he didn't dare move or pick up his books. Then I went home all on my own. I thought *they* were cool, I thought I was just like a disapproving old woman.

Leslie Wilson, *Last Train from Kummersdorf*

- What Nazi stereotype of a Jew are the children taught at school?
- How does the narrative challenge this stereotype?
- Does the boy telling the story do anything to stop the other boys? Why or why not?

Find evidence from the extract for your answers.

Remember

Texts are influenced by the time and place the writer lives in.

We read a text depending on the time and place we live in.

Ideas in texts are not fixed. They change as societies change.

Check your progress

LEVEL 5) I understand how racism affected texts and how they are now read differently

LEVEL 6) I can explain how racism affected texts and how they are now read differently

LEVEL 7) I can analyse how racist and non-racist contexts affect how texts are written and read

This lesson will
- help you recognise different types of sonnets.

Literature isn't just 'made up' by every new writer that comes along. Every writer inherits what has gone before but then uses it in his or her own way and time.

Getting you thinking

If you were serious about your feelings for someone, how would you tell them?

Traditionally, writers have used a poetic form called the 'sonnet' as a way of expressing love. When Romeo first meets Juliet, they speak together in 14 rhymed lines of deep love. They meet 'in' a sonnet. Shakespeare also wrote a series of 154 sonnets to a fair young man and a 'dark lady'. Here is one of them.

It was a convention of the sonnets of Shakespeare's time to compare a woman to a beautiful summer day. How does Shakespeare play with this idea?

Shall I compare thee to a summer's day?
Thou art more lovely and more temperate.
Rough winds do shake the darling buds of May,
And summer's lease hath all too short a date.   4
Sometime too hot the eye of heaven shines,
And often is his gold complexion dimmed;
And every **fair from fair** sometime declines,
By chance, or nature's changing course, **untrimmed**;   8
But thy eternal summer shall not fade,
Nor lose possession of that fair **thou ow'st**,
Nor shall Death brag thou wand'rest in his shade,
When in eternal lines to time thou grow'st.   12
   So long as men can breathe, or eyes can see,
   So long lives this, and this gives life to thee.   14

Glossary

fair from fair: beautiful thing from beauty

untrimmed: divested of ornament, made plain

thou ow'st: you own

1 In groups, take one section each (lines 1–4; 5–8; 9–12; 13–14) and read it closely.

2 Then, join together to answer the following questions:
- 1–8: How is the girl he loves *too* good to compare to a mere summer day?
- 9–14: How, according to Shakespeare, is his poem for her *better* than a mere summer?

How does it work?

The first sonnet – the Italian formation **8, 6** – was invented by the Florentine poet Petrarch (1304–1374) to praise (and blame) his lady-love Laura. He called it a sonneto (a 'little song').

Sir Thomas Wyatt brought the sonnet back to the English court during Henry VIII's reign and soon everyone was writing the fashionable new poem 'for the ladies'. The English formation – **4, 4, 4, 2** – developed because it offers more rhyme choices. (It's easier to rhyme in Italian than in English.)

Both forms of the sonnet have 14 lines, a strict rhyme scheme, and divide into clear sections. However, there are some important differences:

Italian/Petrachan sonnet	English/Shakespearean sonnet
In the Italian sonnet, there is a '**turn**' in the poem after line 8, reinforced by a new pattern of rhymes in lines 9–14.	In the English sonnet, there is a **final couplet** where the argument is clinched, extended or reversed in a dramatic way.
The Italian sonnet is 'a **poem of two halves**' split into eight lines and six lines. The second part 'rejects' the first. (8, 6.)	The English sonnet also has two halves but the rhymes mark these out in **three quatrains** and a brief summarising **couplet**. (4, 4, 4, 2.)
In the Italian version, the **rhymes** (and sometimes the layout) mark a clear break between the first half from the second.	The English version repeats a four-line idea three times and then 'turns' in the conclusion. The **rhyme scheme** (ABAB CDCD EFEF GG) reflects this.
The Italian version complains for eight lines, then turns and accepts that love is worth it.	The English can love and complain together at the same time!

Now you try it APP

Two hundred years later, the poet Wordsworth returns to Petrarch's original **form** – eight lines 'answered' by six – but changes the **content**. His 'little song' describes a passenger leaving Revolutionary France, a black woman deported by new laws.

We had a fellow-Passenger who came
From Calais with us, **gaudy in array**,
A Negro Woman like a Lady gay,
Yet silent as a woman fearing blame;
Dejected, meek, yea pitiably tame,
She sate, from notice turning not away,
But on our **proffer'd** kindness still did lay
A weight of **languid** speech, or at the same
Was silent, motionless in eyes and face.
She was a Negro Woman driv'n from France,
Rejected like all others of that race,
Not one of whom may now find footing there;
This the poor Out-cast did to us declare,
Nor murmur'd at the unfeeling **Ordinance**.

September 1, 1802

Glossary

gaudy in array: wearing brightly coloured clothes

proffer'd: offered

languid: weary (all hope gone)

Ordinance: law

1 In pairs discuss the following:

- What words sum up the woman's state of mind?
- What is the woman's reaction to the law that made her leave France? Is the poet's reaction different?

2 This is a 400-year-old form used for what in 1802 was a news item (the deportation of free black people from France).

- Why does Wordsworth use a 'love poem' form to write about it?
- Can you find two 'halves' formed by rhyme patterns?
- The poem is two sentences. Do they match with the two rhyme sections?

3 Finally, look at the poem's language. Wordsworth's poem is now over two centuries old.

- What words are outdated, altered, quaint or even offensive to a modern reader? Explain why.

> **Remember**
>
> Poets don't always obey the rules!

Development activity

Write a comparison of the two sonnets. Comment on

- their **purpose** (Why was each sonnet written? Is one better suited to the sonnet form than the other? Why?)
- their **form** (What features do they have in common? What features have changed? What would (a) Petrarch and (b) Shakespeare recognise as a sonnet in Wordsworth's poem?).

Check your progress

LEVEL 5 | I can compare sonnet conventions from different periods

LEVEL 6 | I can explore and explain sonnet conventions from different periods

LEVEL 7 | I can analyse two examples from the sonnet tradition

Level Booster

LEVEL 5

- I can compare and contrast conventions in texts
- I can identify texts in context (time, place and social setting)
- I can make some explanation of how contexts (time, place and social settings) affect how texts are read
- I can explain the extent to which context affects how texts are written

LEVEL 6

- I can recognise textual conventions in a literary form
- I can recognise textual conventions in a non-literary form
- I can discuss in some detail how the same literary form is used differently in different periods
- I can discuss in some detail how the meaning of the same text can change over time
- I can discuss in some detail how ideas in texts are treated differently in different times and places

LEVEL 7

- I can begin to analyse how texts are influenced by their literary tradition
- I can begin to analyse how texts are influenced by the context in which they were written
- I can begin to analyse how texts are influenced by the context in which they are read
- I can begin to analyse how a text is interpreted in relation to its society, culture and time

Chapter 7

Longer texts and reading activities

What's it all about?

Bringing all the Assessment Focuses together.

EDITH	Where are you going, darling?
ANNE	I need fresh air. I need to escape. I need to see my beautiful city. Just once more. I need to stretch and breathe the sky.
EDITH	*(humouring her)* Yes, darling. Don't we all.

Anne tries the trapdoor.

	Darling. What are you doing?
ANNE	The empty ballroom of dreams. *(She sings.)*
	Dancing in the dark till the tune ends,
	We're dancing in the dark – and it soon ends –
	We're waltzing in the wonder of why we're here –
	Time hurries by – we're here and gone…

Anne floats into an empty square. Amsterdam at night. There are searchlights and the crump of bombs.

Come, bombs! Come, fire! Devour the Nazi monster. Even destroy my beloved Amsterdam if you have to.

Outside Inside

Outside inside
Two worlds apart
Inside we argue
Outside we part
Inside we're safe
But we fight for a chair
Outside we're taken
To God knows where
Outside inside
Two worlds apart
Inside we argue
Outside the broken heart
And sky and travel and death

Outside the Royal Palace. A man (Dussel) stalks her.

MAN	What are you doing in the streets, child? In the middle of the night?
ANNE	Looking for my childhood.
MAN	But surely you want to grow up?
ANNE	Yes. But I'm afraid. I want life to go backwards.
MAN	Ah yes, I thought you were in pain. Can I tell you about my hobby? I am totally obsessed with military bands. I would follow any band, good or bad, to the ends of the earth and often do in my imagination. As soon as I get home I immediately start the military music on my radiogram. I know every march ever written, almost every band that ever played, their particular style. There in my living-room I march, back and forth, back and forth, every lunch-time, every night. It is a wonderful exercise and I can assure you it is a

morally uplifting and spiritual experience. The Germans are a humane race, compassionate. I know you are afraid because of the things you have heard they have done or are about to do. A lot of this you can disregard. It is propaganda. I maintain that soon you will notice a big change. An occupying power is bound to take actions that seem draconian and excessively harsh early on. The Jews are merely an expediency, a scapegoat for our ambitions. It is almost understandable, even if a little painful. Open up. *(He has become Hitler and wants to probe into **Anne**'s mouth.)* Where's my scalpel?

ANNE   Here!

She takes the knife from his white coat pocket, thrusts it into his stomach.

MAN   Help me! Help me! Heil –

He raises his arm, calling to her, but his cry becomes Hitler's fanatical call to his followers.

      Heil! Heil!

Massed crowds shout 'Heil!' in reply.

ANNE   Hitler's dead. *(She is by the radio.)*

EDITH   *(coming to **Anne**)* What are you doing up, this time of night?

ANNE   Mother! *(She whispers in **Edith**'s ear.)*

EDITH   What?

ANNE   It's true! It's true!

AF 2   What two stage directions make it clear that Amsterdam is a city at war when Anne emerges through the trap-door?

AF 3   Would you describe this play as naturalistic? You may wish to consider
- the role of song/music
- the appearance and behaviour of the man – Dussel
- how Anne behaves
- the title of the play and how it relates to what happens.

AF 4   Why is the man's long speech important to this scene as a whole? Consider:
- how he changes as it progresses
- the underlying message about the 'actions' the Germans are taking towards Jewish people.

AF 5   Comment on the different/contrasting language and actions in this scene. Find two examples and explain the effect of them on the audience.

AF 6   Comment on the writer's overall viewpoint in this scene. What do you think he/she is trying to say about
- childhood
- the effect of the war on ordinary people?

AF 7   To what extent is the play's success dependent on knowing about what happened in World War 2 and the knowledge that Anne Frank was a real person? Write two paragraphs explaining your point of view.

The Brooke urgently needs your help to save working animals from suffering – and help the poor families who depend on them too. Right now, millions of animals carry heavy loads, such as building materials and produce. Without their help, poor families struggle to earn a living, but many don't know how to care for their donkeys and horses properly.

The Brooke's local experts treat animals when they are sick or injured – and educate owners in better animal care, saving donkeys and horses from terrible pain.

For your FREE inspiration pack and DVD, showing our work in action, visit www.helpboth.org, fill in the form below or text 'BROOKE G' to 80010*

*Each message sent to us is charged at your standard network SMS rate only. Reply STOP at any time to opt out of receiving FREE information about the Brooke, but we don't spam!

The Brooke Broadmead House
21 Panton Street London SWTY 4DR.

The animal charity that helps people too

The Brooke – Founded by Dorothy Brooke in 1934

Title _____

Name _____

Surname _____

Address _____

_____

_____

Postcode _____

Tel _____

Email _____

Please write your email address above if you would be happy to receive emails from the Brooke about our activities and work with animals overseas (you can unsubscribe easily at any time).

AF 2   What two roles does the Brooke charity have? Make sure you find appropriate quotations to support your answer.

AF 3   The leaflet implies a number of things about how charities work best – what do you think these are, and do you agree?

AF 4   How well does the structure of the leaflet work? Comment in particular on

- the juxtaposition of particular words and images with each other
- the layout and order in which our eye is drawn to particular words or images
- the different ways the text – or words in the text – are presented.

AF 5   Comment on the ways the writer uses language to achieve a particular effect. Consider:

- the style and structure of the main text used with the image
- features of persuasive language used in the text below the image

Make sure you include carefully selected quotations or references to support your point of view.

AF 6   'The text as a whole has several purposes, but this is a weakness as much as a strength'. Comment on this statement, making detailed reference to the text.

Daylight confirmed the impression which I had felt the night before, of there being too many trees at Blackwater. The house is stifled by them. They are, for the most part, young and planted much too thickly. On a nearer view, the garden proved to be small and poor and ill-kept. I left it behind me, opened a little gate in a ring fence, and found myself in a plantation of fir trees. After a walk of about half a mile, the path took a sudden turn and I found myself suddenly on the margin of a vast open space and looking down at the Blackwater lake from which the house takes its name.

The ground shelving away below me, was all sand, with a few little heathy hillocks to break the monotony of it. The lake itself had evidently once flowed to the spot on which I stood, and had gradually been wasted and dried up to less than a third of its former size. I saw its still, stagnant waters, a quarter of a mile away from me in the hollow separated into pools and ponds, by twinning reeds and rushes and little knolls of earth.

On the farther bank from me, the trees rose thickly again, and shut out the view and cast their black shadows on the sluggish, shallow water. As I walked down to the lake, I saw that the ground on its farther side was damp and marshy, overgrown with rank grass and dismal willows. The water, which was clear enough on the open sandy side, where the sun shone, looked black and poisonous opposite to me, where it lay deeper under the shade of the spongy banks and the rank overhanging thickets and tangled trees. The frogs were croaking, and the rats were slipping in and out of the shadowy water, like live shadows themselves, as I got nearer to the marshy side of the lake.

I saw here, lying half in and half out of the water, the rotten wreck of an old overturned boat, with a sickly spot of sunlight glimmering through a gap in the trees on its dry surface, and a snake basking in the midst of this spot, fantastically coiled and treacherously still. Far and near, the view suggested the same dreary impression of solitude and decay; and the glorious brightness of the summer sky overhead, seemed only to deepen and harden the gloom and barrenness of the wilderness on which it shone.

I turned and retraced my steps to the high, healthy ground; directing them a little aside from my former path, towards a shabby old wooden shed, which stood on the outer skirt of the fir plantation, and which I had not noticed before.

On approaching the shed, I found that it had once been a boathouse, and that an attempt had been apparently made to convert it afterwards into a sort of rude arbour, by placing inside it a firwood seat, a few stools and a table. I entered the place and sat down for a while, to rest and get my breath again.

I had not been in the boathouse more than a minute, when it struck me that the sound of my own quick breathing was very strangely echoed by something beneath me. I listened intently for a moment and heard a low, thick, sobbing breath that seemed to come from the ground under the seat which I was occupying. My nerves are not easily shaken; but on this occasion, I started to my feet in a fright – called out – received no answer – summoned back my recreant courage and looked under the seat.

AF 2 In what ways is 'Blackwater Lake' an appropriate name for the lake which the narrator comes across? Find at least three references taken from **both** the third and the fourth paragraphs.

AF 3 There are a number of vivid descriptions of trees in the text (for example, the trees at the house itself and the trees on the opposite bank of the lake). How are these trees described, and what atmosphere do they create?

AF 4 Why does the writer introduce the boathouse at this point in the text rather than at the beginning, before the narrator had walked down to the lake? Think about what we are told **before** he reaches the shed, and the atmosphere that has been built up.

AF 5 It might be said that the writer describes things as if through a camera lens.

- Can you find at least one example when he describes a large, wide view of things, and one example when he focuses very carefully on a close-up detail?
- How do these descriptions contribute to the overall atmosphere created?

AF 6
AF 7 In your opinion, what **type** or **genre** of text do you think this is? Support your viewpoint with evidence from the text itself, making reference to similar texts if you wish.

The death of handwriting impoverishes us

Melanie McDonagh believes keyboards can never reveal the personality of the author

Melanie McDonagh, *Daily Telegraph*, 27 Feb 2009

My daughter's birth certificate came as a nasty shock. For as long as I could remember, state certificates in Ireland were filled in by the same class of clerk: people with conscientious, neat handwriting, which bore all the stamp of having been taught by nuns. But the world has changed. My child's certificate was computer generated, and bore no nice signature from the registrar. There was one from me, but as it had originally been written on one of those digital screens that delivery men use, it was an unrecognisable scrawl. So, no personal touch there then.

That's the way things are going. In her soon-to-be-published book, entitled *Script and Scribble: A Defence of Penmanship*, the American author Kitty Burns Florey contends that handwriting is becoming a lost art. By the next generation it will, she says, have gone the way of Nineveh and Tyre: 'There's a widespread belief that, in a digital world, forming letters on paper with a pen is pointless and obsolete… I am part of the last generation for whom handwriting was taught as a vital skill.' She was prompted to write the book when she discovered that handwriting in some schools was being replaced by keyboarding instruction. She concluded that, in the near future, handwriting will only be used by people who keep a diary. 'I suspect,' she says, 'that there are people today who have never received a letter written on paper and mailed in an envelope with a stamp.'

The obvious question is, does it matter? I'm someone who has gone from writing naturally with pen in hand, to now only being able to think fluently in front of a keyboard. If I tried to construct this article on paper, I couldn't do it. When it comes to letters, of course I write them – quite nicely, if I do it with a dip pen and ink – but emails come easier. One reason why older people write letters to newspapers, while young people comment online, is that younger people don't think on to paper any more. And undoubtedly, they are more legible when chasing a flashing cursor across a screen.

There can be no doubt that we are witnessing the creation of the first keyboard generation. Just over two years ago, a US study of 1.5 million 16 and 17 year olds found that only 15 per cent of them used joined-up writing. Most used block capitals – baby writing. Over here, about a third of boys and a quarter of girls don't reach the Government's required standard by the age of 11, and anyway, the National Literacy Strategy doesn't require those that do to use old-fashioned cursive script. And, by God, you can tell.

It is the most significant development since the working class stopped putting crosses instead of signatures, and I'd say it's a dehumanising trend. For a few years, I worked with medieval manuscripts. And although I wasn't much good at **palaeography**, I rather got to love the way one hand would differ from another. There were quirks, little cartoons in margins – including rude ones – funny little fingers drawn on the side identifying passages of interest, flourishes and the signs of haste. There was an immediacy between writer and reader which could make the centuries vanish. And I remember the horrible shock when I moved from manuscript books to early printed ones.

What! No little pictures, no underlinings? Everything the same? Gross.

Well, that's pretty well where we're at if the written word goes out of fashion. We'll still be communicating, but one essential aspect will be absent: the personality that is invested in the writing. **Graphology** may be a dud science, but on an everyday basis our writing does say something about who we are. If we lose one of the three Rs, we'll be the poorer for it.

AF 2 The writer provides both personal experience and separate factual information as evidence of what has happened to handwriting in recent years. Identify one example of each from different parts of the text.

AF 3
AF 6 The writer says that the way handwriting is disappearing is creating the first 'keyboard generation' and is a 'dehumanising trend'. Explain what you think she means by these two phrases, and whether you agree with her.

AF 4 How does the final paragraph sum up the writer's overall viewpoint about handwriting?

AF 5 The writer uses language in different ways to draw the reader into what she is saying. Find and comment on the impact of at least two of the following:
- the use of informal or chatty language
- the use of questions
- the use short, snappy sentences or phrases after longer, more reflective ones
- the detailed description of handwriting in medieval manuscripts
- the use of personal pronouns, such as 'our', 'us', 'we'.

Glossary

palaeography: the study of handwriting and manuscripts of the past

Graphology: the study of handwriting, especially to analyse the writer's character

FINAL CHAPTER?

With World Book Day happening this week, Michael Parker investigates whether the humble paperback is under threat from eBooks.

Five-and-a-half centuries since Johannes Guttenberg developed the printing press and Aldo Manuzio invented the pocket-size book, words are now cheaper, quicker and easier to print than ever before.

Hundreds of millions of books are printed every year across the globe, and whilst wood block and moveable type gave way to phototypesetting and digital printing, the printed book remains a useful relic, a perfect-bound dinosaur. Popular in their day, the papyrus scroll, wax tablet, cassette and video tape have all fallen to new, better technology – and yet the book clings stubbornly on. But, in a new digital age where computers can easily send exact digital copies silently and swiftly around the world in seconds, is the book's days numbered?

For some, eBooks and screen readers are the future: a place where bookworms will carry dozens if not hundreds of books stored digitally for reading on handheld devices. Perhaps strangely, the world's largest bookseller, Amazon, is leading the charge with its Kindle eBook reader. Just over a year old, the Kindle can access through its internet connection a library of 185,000 books, newspapers and magazines. Though it has gained much media attention, it is not the first of its kind. Current competitors include the iRex iLiad and Sony Reader, while Franklin released its first eBookMan reader as long ago as 1999.

Jeff Bezos, Amazon's chief executive, says he believes eBooks will not shrink Amazon's profits – indeed, Kindle-owners are book-lovers, he told shareholders last year, who will now buy eBooks as well as printed versions.

It is the comforting presence of a book that stops many from switching to screen readers. For millions of us that spend our working lives staring at computer screens, the prospect of indulging their hobby on yet another screen hardly appeals. But the so called 'electronic link' screens of modern eBooks reflect light like a matt, printed page, dispensing with the back-lighting of computer screens that can tire a reader's eyes. Devices even allow you to scribble notes in the margins or 'dog-ear' pages.

After all, the market has already shown it can prefer convenience over quality – though die-hard fans still champion the aural superiority of vinyl records or CDs, the inferior but more portable MP3 has triumphed over all others. For many, the convenience of eBooks will win over romantic notions related to musty page-turning. And screen readers may appeal where those musty books do not – perhaps to younger audiences.

But the technology is also its own Achilles' heel. Yet mirroring the High Definition-DVD vs Blu-ray or VHS vs Betamax wars, competing file formats have split the market and make a single universal eBook format unlikely. This is partly because of a desire for DRM – digital rights management software – that prevents users from passing a purchased eBook to anyone else, or even to another device, such as a computer, owned by the same person. While Amazon's proprietary AZW format may try to protect copyright holders' (and its own) income, it also locks eBooks purchased in that format, meaning that customers can only download on to Kindle devices or future Amazon products. Those with long memories point to how quickly DRM in music and DVDs were discarded as obstructive and unworkable.

Converts are confident that teething problems will pass. Mark Rusher of Orion Publishing said: "I was unsure at first, but it;s convenient, easy to use and saves on paper. My daughter uses one too, and I have to remember that her generation are so familiar with reading on screen, it comes as second nature. It's only a matter of time before retailers cotton on. At the moment, buying is still hit-and-miss and not all formats are compatible, but I see no reason why they won't really take off."

Jason Epstein, former editorial director of Random House publishers, has a vision of a "book ATM" where a digital eBook file is printed, bound and presented to the customer in minutes. This would generate profits for copyright-holders and publishers, offering access to a far larger catalogue than a bookshop could hold, while still giving the consumer the physical book they crave.

That inventors would rather distil choices from vast digital libraries into a physical book form, and that after 10 years eBook have made negligible progress, shows the strength of the book's hold on us. When the last AA battery has died and the last electrical outlet gone dark, books will still be recording tales and sharing ideas long into the future.

World Book Day is on March 5. For more information, go to www.worldbookday.com

AF 2 What factual information do we learn about the Kindle ebook reader in the third paragraph?

AF 3 Read from paragraph 5 to the end of the article. Find two examples of advantages ebooks have over traditional texts, and two disadvantages.

AF 4 Comment on the title of the article and the tag-line underneath. How effective and appropriate are these in terms of summing up what the article is about?

AF 5 The traditional book is described in a number of ways by the writer throughout the text. Explain what the overall effect of these descriptions is, and why you think the writer used them.
- 'comforting physical presence'
- 'the book clings stubbornly on'
- 'a useful relic, a perfect-bound dinosaur'

AF 6 Read the final paragraph of the article.
- What is the future for the book according to the writer?
- What powerful image does he use to support his point of view?

Aunt Julia

Aunt Julia spoke Gaelic
very loud and very fast.
I could not answer her –
I could not understand her.

She wore men's boots
when she wore any.
– I can see her strong foot,
stained with peat,
paddling with the treadle of the spinning wheel
while her right hand drew yarn
marvellously out of the air.

Hers was the only house
where I've lain at night
in the absolute darkness
of a box bed, listening to
crickets being friendly.

She was buckets
and water flouncing into them.
She was winds pouring wetly
round house-ends.
She was brown eggs, black skirts
and a keeper of threepennybits
in a teapot.

Aunt Julia spoke Gaelic
very loud and very fast.
By the time I had learned
a little, she lay
silenced in the absolute black
of a sandy grave
at Luskentyre.

But I hear her still, welcoming me
with a seagull's voice
across a hundred yards
of peatscrapes and lazybeds
and getting angry, getting angry
with so many questions
unanswered.

AF 2 A number of phrases or lines in the poem suggest that Aunt Julia's house was in a country rather than town setting. Find at least two, and explain why you selected them.

AF 3 Although the poet does not say what age he was when he stayed with his aunt, how does he imply that he was a child? Think about:
- the relationship between them
- the way in which the 'story' of the poem is told
- any other details the poet reveals.

Make sure you refer closely to actual words, lines or phrases from the poem.

AF 4 A number of verses link or repeat ideas or language in the poem. Which verses are linked, and what do you think the effect of this linking is? Consider:
- repeated lines or phrases
- linked situations or descriptions.

AF 5 How does the poet use powerful imagery to convey Aunt Julia's physical appearance and movements?

AF 6 Do you think that the poet enjoyed staying at his aunt's? Explain your opinion with close reference to the poem.

AF 7 What evidence is there from the poem that this is set in a particular culture, and a time different from our own today? Think about:
- dialect words
- reference to pastimes or activities
- names of places.

Teacher Guide

Where the final task of the double-page section is substantial enough to provide a snapshot of students' progress, this has been marked as an **APP opportunity**.

Each double-page section ends with a **Check your progress** box. This offers a levelled checklist against which students can self- or peer-assess their final piece of writing from the **Development** or, occasionally, **Now you try it** section.

The end of chapter **Level Booster** is a less task-specific checklist of the skills students need to master to reach Level 5, 6 and 7. It can be used to help students see the level they are working at currently and to visualise what they need to do to make progress.

To the Teacher

The general aim of these books is the practical and everyday application of **Assessment for Learning (AfL)**: to ensure every child knows how they are doing and what they need to do to improve. The specific aim is to support **APP (Assessing Pupils' Progress)**: the 'periodic' view of progress by teacher and learner.

The books empower the student by modelling the essential skills needed at each level, and by allowing them to practise and then demonstrate independently what they know and can do across every reading and writing (APP) strand. They support the teacher by providing opportunities to gather and review secure evidence of progress in each **Assessment Focus (AF)**. Where appropriate (and especially at lower levels) the books facilitate teacher **scaffolding** of such learning and assessment.

The series offers exercises that we hope will not only help students add descriptive power and nuance to their vocabulary but also expand the grammatical constructions they can access and use: above all, the ability to write and read in sentences (paragraphs, texts) – to think consciously in complete thoughts.

We hope we can enrich the way students read, recognising not just the texts they are decoding but also the contexts in which they read them. Our extracts cannot replace longer texts. The longer reading passages in Chapter 7 of our Reading books, with questions that cover all the AFs working together, are a crucial acknowledgement of this. Each AF is a provisional isolation of various emphases, to be practised and mastered before bringing it back to the real reading and writing of whole texts in which all these – suitably polished – skills can be applied.

Gareth Calway

Series Editor

1 Summarise and synthesise information

Getting you thinking

It might help to photocopy the travel brochure extract for students, so they can highlight or underline the relevant sections about Marrakesh.

How does it work?

- This text is a travel brochure. It really tries to 'sell' you Marrakesh as a holiday destination. Marrakesh is referred to once in paragraph 1, once in paragraph 2 and throughout paragraph 3.

- Paragraph 1 uses lavish descriptions full of colour and detail, with rich nouns and adjectives like 'romance' and 'ochre-coloured', and suggestive, alliterative phrases like 'full of myths and mystery'. The poetic language implies that it will be a rewarding experience.

- The paragraph 2 reference is more down to earth but reassures the traveller, making the journey to Marrakesh sound problem free and the stay luxurious, 'On arrival a coach will take you to the four-star Hotel Asni'.

- The description in paragraph 3 attracts the reader because it is so vividly and visually described.

Phrases such as 'a labyrinth of tiny alleyways, which team with street life' make the place sound busy and lively. The word 'labyrinth' makes it sound mysterious and exciting.

- To summarise, according to this brochure, Marrakesh has a varied array of attractions from palaces to famous markets. The hotel provides luxurious accommodation, and a wide range of historical and cultural excursions are available.

Development

You could ask the students to carry out the following activities.

- Choose a country or city that interests you. Investigate how the place or city has been described in various types of texts such as travel guides, novels, poetry and travel writing. Do you notice any similarities or differences?

- Consider the area in which you live. How would you describe it if you were trying to sell it as a holiday location? How would this be different if you were describing it in some non-fiction travel writing?

2 Select and explore evidence from different texts

Getting you thinking

There are a number of lines students might choose to support A. These could include 'burnt-out ends of smoky days' and 'grimy scraps.' They should give reasons for their choices. For C, students should find evidence for descriptions of and references to smells, sounds and sights. To support D, students should notice the 'lighting of the lamps' and the 'cab-horse.' They will find little to support B.

How does it work?

Students will note the way loneliness is conveyed:

- by **the word 'lonely' itself.** (Look at where it is used – notice that it both describes an object and has a general effect on the emotion of the poem.)

- through **images or details that convey that mood:** 'withered leaves', 'vacant lots', 'burnt-out … days'. (All the objects in the poem are described as empty or forlorn; even the leaves have decayed. The air of hopelessness is reinforced by the weather.)

- by **the weary rhythm and tone:** 'The showers beat/On broken blinds'.

- by **the absence of people** in the poem (actions such as 'the lighting of the lamps' are performed anonymously; the only traces of human life are the 'smells of steaks in passageways' and the abandoned 'newspapers'; a cab waits but nobody gets into it).

Students should pick up that the poem is meant to convey loneliness. The light 'spreads darkly down' suggests a weary tone. Even the light is dark! The use of the words 'silence' and 'loneliness' suggest emptiness, a lack of human activity. This is backed up by the 'empty' chairs and the description of the empty dining room. The 'shoeless corridors' also suggest that nobody is around. The porter is still there but he is alone and reading, to pass the time. The only thing that is full is the ashtray.

3 Make relevant points clearly identified with apt quotations

Getting you thinking

Share students' answers, modelling particularly effective use of quotation on the board. Alternatively, show students how this student has answered the question. Emphasise that she has picked out key pieces of detail, including a short quotation. She has explained each quotation well, discussing its effect on the reader.

The writer builds up tension by describing the start of the race in minute detail. The flag is described in detail, it 'fluttered more gently now', and this makes the reader feel as though they are experiencing the tense wait themselves through Bannister's eyes. The writer slows down his description in several places, for instance, when he thinks about an exciting moment from a play ('Saint Joan flashed through my mind'). This builds up tension as it delays the actual start of the race and shows Bannister's excitement and expectation.

Development

Ask students to carry out the following task:

Imagine somebody is writing their autobiography and has asked you for advice in describing a key moment of their life. Use Branson's and Bannister's extracts to compile five top tips for making their incident sound interesting to the reader. For example:

> **Number 1** Include plenty of detail, as this makes it seem realistic and helps the reader imagine they are there.

4 Understand how a line of argument is developed

How does it work?

Look at the two student answers with the class. Draw out from them that Response A is better than B because it traces the writer's argument by focusing on apt evidence from the text. It focuses on a single word and analyses its impact, explaining how the word is usually used. Response B uses a whole line of quotation and, as a result, the analysis is less focused.

Now you try it

The argument is that there is no excuse for not being able to cope when the situation was

1 entirely predictable
2 costing the country an unnecessary £1.2 billion in lost labour
3 much better than 1963
4 not as bad as the Blitz, through which transport was maintained
5 avoidable if roads had been gritted
6 avoidable if severe weather warnings had been heeded.

The conclusion makes it clear that the writer thinks transport bosses are to blame.

Development

1 Students should pick up that the writer thinks the transport authorities are to blame.
2 Students should work out that the first article is blaming nobody. It is pointing out that the snow is the heaviest it has been for 18 years.

1 Make inferences from challenging texts

How does it work?

Point out to your class that the sample answer deserves a Level 6 because the student has engaged with the poem and thoroughly answered both questions. The student is able to identify different layers of meaning. The student has recognised irony and backed up his idea by quoting from the text. He has also noted the real meaning behind the poem, which is that the poet's efforts to be well prepared have 'ended in failure.'

Development

As an extension, ask students:

- Why do you think the poet adopts a persona in the poem?
- What does this choice imply about the narrator? What would you infer about a narrator who adopts the persona of a worm or a rat?

2 Interpret key points from different parts of texts

Now you try it

It would be helpful to photocopy the *Romeo and Juliet* extract, quite large, for students so they can mark in their directions. Students could begin by reading the dialogue in pairs, each playing a part and thinking about how their character might act.

Romeo and Juliet's dialogue here is a sonnet. The legendary lovers meet at a party, probably on a dance floor, and their first dialogue is a **shared** love poem, full of holy words.

Help students to understand what is happening by prompting them: What is Romeo angling for? What is Juliet's initial – and eventual – response?

This love proves fatal to both at the end of the play. Ask students to look up the words 'pilgrim' and 'shrine' and list all possible meanings. Do they get any hints from these meanings about the 'path of true love' or its fatal end? What do they infer from the word 'shrine' and how might that affect the way we read 'pilgrim', 'saint' and other 'holy' words?

Development

When students have completed their answers, they should use them to answer this question: 'What change is implied in Romeo and Juliet's relationship from the beginning to the end of the extract?'

They should write a paragraph with evidence from the extract for their response.

3 Consider the wider implications of themes, events and ideas in texts

Getting you thinking

Students should point out that in Bradford the police are not used to seeing homeless people sleeping rough, so the homeless are moved on. The boy has no sleep. People hardly ever give money to the homeless.

How does it work?

This is what you should be looking for in answer to the Getting you thinking questions.

1 The boy wants to be inconspicuous and to be left alone. In Bradford the boy was 'getting moved on every hour' so he prefers to be homeless in London. This implies that the police in London are desensitised because the problem is so great.

2 We can deduce that the boy is pretty savvy. He is realistic about London: he 'knew the streets … weren't paved with gold'. The repetition of 'knew' implies this. He is also aware that he will be one of 'thousands … sleeping rough and begging for coppers', not an isolated case.

He perceives London to offer something better, a chance to improve his life.

Now you try it

Students should have noted that:

1 London offers a new beginning.
London offers new opportunities.
You have a clean sheet – nobody knows you.

2 London is not paved with gold.
Thousands sleep rough.

3 He can start again.

4 Bradford (by implication) is a place where nothing happens. He does not see Bradford as big/fast/full of opportunities.
In Bradford you cannot invent your own past. He was and is known there.

4 Explore the connotations of words and images

How does it work?

Feed back students' answers. Draw out the following points:

- 'Sinuous' is horribly snake-like. Breakfast suits the time of day and there is almost a hint that the girls might be its next mouthful. The stone ball crushed like a malteser **denotes** the demolition of this part of the old school gate. The same applies to the drainpipes becoming macaroni (food again!). But both **connote** a world where huge forces are crushing the very structures of the girls' world.

- The atmosphere is both funny and frightening – even famously chin-up Miss Bowker feels fragile. The threat seems bigger than just having to use the loos in a boys' school because the text is working at a deeper level of meaning (through the images). It conveys a deep level of menace, the horror they either imagine or actually will face in 'Harvest Road boys' school'.

Now you try it

It would be useful to share the following terms with students as they come to read and analyse the passage:

- **pathetic fallacy:** where something non-human (like weather or scenery) represents a human emotion: as when a storm accompanies a murder in horror stories

- **transferred epithets:** where a descriptive word is transferred from a human to a non-human object (for example, the hump-backed bridge here cannot feel misery: it is the girls in the marching column who feel miserable).

Feed back students' responses to each image:

- 'A miserable little hump-backed bridge' – this helps to conjure up a feeling of foreboding.

- 'a solitary railway-line' – the railway-line stands alone. It is 'empty and rusting' which suggests it is disused. The end of the line for the girls.

- Houses 'afflicted by some dreadful disease' completes the picture of foreboding and increases the girls' dread as they approach the boys' school. The very place appears unwelcoming and almost sick.

The mood created is a depressing one. The weather is cold and windy (again using personification). This again suggests the boys' school would be unwelcoming and possibly hostile. 'Funereal' suggests death and decay.

Development

Ask students to look at events from another point of view. How might the boys be feeling about the imminent arrival of these strange girls at their school? Imagine the headmaster of old Harvest Road boys' school has told the boys that the girls are entering his school for a while.

The boys were hunched over the football. They were grim faced and serious.

'We won't be playing British Bulldog now, will we?' said Terry.

'Or football,' added Jimmy.

The headmaster appeared on the playground like an apparition. He was wearing his long black raincoat and the damp made his grey hair stand on end, like a ghostly crown. He stroked his long pointed chin, as he always did when thinking. He strode up to the boys like a military leader. Like he was Napoleon ordering the retreat from Moscow.

'You know, Terry, it won't be too bad. When you're older, just a bit older, you'll be glad to know some of these girls.'

The headmaster spoke in a low, gravelly voice. He seemed the same but his eyes were dull. Rumour had it that he disliked Miss Bowker and the way she does things.

Ask students to work in pairs to decide what kind of atmosphere is built up in this extract.

5 Explore what can be inferred from the finer details of texts

How does it work?

Model the detailed student response to what is inferred from the text. It is aiming at a strong Level 6. Ask students to write down why they think this response received a good level. Then go through these points:

- It analyses information and makes comments on some finer details of the text.
- It is clear and easy to understand what the student thinks.

- It shows that the student has read the text carefully and it makes detailed inferences about characters and their relationships.
- It 'embeds' quotations effectively into different sentences.

Development

Tell students they should think about what is stated literally and what is implied by the writer about his upbringing. Students should prepare a one-minute presentation to give to the class on the **detailed inferences** that they have made about this.

Chapter 3 AF4 Identify and comment on the structure and organisation of texts

---

1 Comment on how successfully writers have opened their stories

Getting you thinking

Ask students to decide which story opening they like best and why.

How does it work?

The writer of A introduces us to an engaging **character** with words like 'slowly rose to his feet' and 'malignant', which suggest that this is someone in a powerful position, who may be evil. The **dialogue** that follows helps the writer to show not tell – in other words, to create a feeling of observation and immediacy. A **conflict** or problem is suggested which immediately grabs our attention as we want to know what crime the other character has been accused of, what s/he will say and what will happen next.

The writer of B establishes a **setting** for the readers by referring to City Cemetery. The **genre** is indicated by the choice of location and the words 'haunted' and 'Halloween'. The beginnings of the **plot** are also made clear as a boy's disappearance is mentioned. This gains the readers' interest as we will want to know what has happened to William Armbruster and why.

Now you try it

Allow students to work in pairs. They should take notes and be willing to defend their decisions.

Development

Students should work out that if we see the story from Detective Whittier's point of view, it is likely that a crime will have been committed and that he will lead an investigation by interviewing witnesses. The story will probably end in an arrest.

If we see the story from Mrs Brenner's point of view, it is likely that she will want to hide something from the detective. It could be that she has murdered her husband and the reasons for doing so will be explored.

2 Explore how writers structure a whole text

Getting you thinking

This article is taken from the Life Advice section of *Cosmo Girl online*. Ask students what this might tell us about the writer's purpose.

How does it work?

The purpose of the article, as the title suggests, is to understand and appreciate home. The article moves from uncertainty over the definition of home, to an ending where a clear appreciation of home (New York) is shown.

The article engages the reader's interest by

- establishing the topic of home (which everyone can relate to) at the start
- using **colloquial** language and a conversational **tone**, and including phrases such as 'I have to be honest', which make us feel like we are confidants
- addressing questions to readers (the first paragraph is full of **rhetorical questions**)
- using the **pronoun** 'you' to appeal to readers directly
- using the **first person** to make it more accessible for readers.

The article establishes a clear theme by

- using the opening **topic sentence** to name the focus of article – definitions of home
- using a **title** that indicates the theme

- **reiterating the theme** throughout ('where I feel the most at home', 'escape campus to come into the city', 'man, I missed them when I was in Europe!', 'it's good to be home').

The article builds toward a conclusion by developing ideas and **sequencing paragraphs** to support this build up:

- **Start: explaining** why the writer once had difficulty defining home and why she now opts for a simple 'New York' response
- **Middle: describing** New York and experiences of it in the past
- **End: returning to a particular experience in the present** in last paragraph.

Now you try it

Remind students about topic sentences and ask them to point out the first two.

Allow students to work in pairs. They should be able to pick out the central idea and work out why it is repeated. They should be able to work out the tone and point out the rhetorical questions, explaining how the use of rhetorical questions develops the theme. Check this by asking some pairs to report back to the class.

Development

Students should plan their article using bullet points or a spider diagram, thinking about everything they have learned in the lesson.

3 Recognise and discuss the effect of a range of structural features in a text

Getting you thinking

If necessary, highlight that George Eliot was a woman, writing in a previous century and long dead! This adds to the humour and shows us that Adrian Mole still has much to learn before he becomes an intellectual.

How does it work?

Draw out with students that the main structural features are **stage directions** (including references to **music** and **sound effects** and the position of characters on stage), **narration** (by the central character) and **juxtaposition** (like the juxtaposition of the lecture and its

disappointment with the flashback to New Year's Eve). All of these features are used to give us a sense of Adrian Mole's character and, in particular, of the gap between his imagination and reality.

The **directions**, written in italics, indicate that **sound** is used before any visual medium. The Mole overture is a piece of music that repeats throughout the play. Here it immediately establishes a comical **atmosphere**. When Adrian moves **front stage** and addresses the audience directly, the focus is placed firmly on him as the key **character**. The playwright **juxtaposes** the music with the appearance of Adrian Mole in order to set up a link between this music and this key character.

This character is also acting as a **narrator** (like the **chorus** in Ancient Greek theatre). Through his words we learn about him and his ambitions. We get the impression that he is a rather self-involved and intellectual character. He also establishes his family **context** and **setting**. It is clear that Adrian has negative feelings towards other characters; he feels disadvantaged by his dull and embarrassing family and wishes for a more intellectual life.

The playwright **juxtaposes** Adrian's pretensions with the deflated reality of his existence through her directions – the lights go up to reveal a remembered scene of a New Year's Eve party – a **flashback**. The lights expose Adrian to us not as the wannabe intellectual who opened the play but as an all too ordinary teenage boy. This changes our picture of him and helps achieve the playwright's aim of gently mocking his pretensions. We literally see him in a different light…

Development

Characters develop through a text but there must also be continuity. It would be unrealistic for a character to become another person entirely. At this key moment of the play, Adrian is still comically pompous but he has partly come to terms with his (ordinary) life.

4 Comment on writers' use of narrative structure to shape meaning

Getting you thinking

Students should be aware that Sade's memories of the past are presented in italics.

How does it work?

Feed back students' ideas. Draw out with students that in this extract, Naidoo:

- shows how confused Sade is feeling by including a **flashback** to an event earlier in her life, so that when she's being interrogated about events in the video shop, she remembers the last time police came to her house in Nigeria

- uses this device of a **flashback** and the **change in tense** from past to present tense to show the difference in time between the two events – one actual and one remembered. The present tense signals to readers that this is a flashback and it also makes the memory more immediate for readers

- makes clear the fears that Sade feels because she associates her current experience with the police in London with her previous experience of them in Nigeria

- provides readers with **backstory**, which helps to fill in gaps in plot. In the sentence 'Frozen inside and out', the writer suggests the way time replays itself for Sade.

Now you try it

Explain to students that a **saga** is a very long story, for example the entire life-history of a hero. **Mini sagas** attempt to suggest a whole story – even a whole life – in 50 words. A lot is suggested by a little, rather than elaborated in detail. Mini sagas should 'expand in your mind like something with water added', as a recent Radio 4 mini saga competition judge put it. **Sagas** tell the history of great heroes, dynasties or great nations. Ask students to consider if writers who choose a **mini-saga narrative** structure are shaping a different content by doing so: the idea of everyday stories of 'little' people, but who are just as heroic in their own way.

Development

Students think about the way past and present events are presented together.

5 Compare the organisation and development of a theme through a whole text

Getting you thinking

An Italian sonnet 'turns' at the end of line 8 – the 'volta' – into a reversal of the ideas expressed in the first eight lines. Ask pupils to identify the word(s) that signals any such change in line 9.

How does it work?

Explain in discussion with students that the form and structure of this poem contribute to its meaning in many subtle ways.

Draw out the following ideas:

- The poem is written in the form of a **sonnet**, a 14-line poem with a strict rhyme and rhythm.
- The rhythm is **iambic pentameter**, made up of five unstressed and five stressed beats per line – di dum di dum di dum di dum di dum, with any variation from this done for effect.
- The **rhyme scheme** here is abbaabbacddece.
- The choice of sonnet form is appropriate given the themes in this poem: love and death.
- The use of enjambment in the poem perhaps reflects the way the poem serves as a journey towards a better understanding of both these themes.
- In line 9 Rossetti provides a **turn** or **volta**, with the word 'yet' suggesting a change in direction. She moves from talking about being remembered to being forgotten before concluding with the idea that it is better for her to be forgotten and her lover to be happy than she be remembered and her lover be sad.

The sentiment being expressed relates to the idea of being at peace with loss. The sounds in the poem reflect this idea as they are made up of soft 's' and 'l' **consonants** and soothing **assonance**. This sets the quiet, solemn **mood** of the poem. The poet also uses repetition to provide a soft hymn-like **tone**, and the rhyme suggests the idea of unity – concord rather than discord.

Now you try it

Ask students:

- What do you think the lack of full rhyme – in lines 2 and 4, and perhaps also 5 and 7 – could suggest in this poem?
- What might the sparsity of language suggest about the nature of the love being described?
- Can you see any comparisons between this poem and Rossetti's in terms of the language that the two poets use?

Draw out in discussion the similarities and differences between Dickinson's poem and Rossetti's:

- Like Rossetti's poem, Dickinson's poem is written in the **first person**, which makes it sound like a personal account.
- In Dickinson's poem, two **quatrain stanzas** describe what is left behind with the lover – the first is 'a legacy of love' and the second is 'boundaries of pain'.
- Dickinson uses alternately rhyming lines – with an alternate rhythm of **iambic tetrameter** (eight-syllable lines) and **iambic trimeter** (six-syllable lines), a classical **ballad** form.

> ## Chapter 4 AF5 Explain and comment on writers' use of language, including grammatical and literary features at word and sentence level

1 Identify and comment on emotive language

Getting you thinking

Model one example for students. Point out to students that they might have chosen 'choirs of wailing shells'. Choirs would be seen as peaceful singing in churches before the war. Now, they are associated with instruments of death. Ask the students to work in pairs to find other emotive words and phrases.

How does it work?

In the first half of this poem, Wilfred Owen suggests that war is insane – 'demented': young men are slaughtered 'as cattle'; it is all a 'monstrous' mockery. This is likely to make the reader feel outrage.

Now you try it

- Students should work out that the girls are girlfriends, young wives, or girls from the soldiers' villages.
- Many of the soldiers had no graves. Thousands were killed in one day and their bodies were left in no-man's land. The 'patient minds' could be the parents of the dead soldiers. They might be unaware of the death of their son, or accepting of the fact.
- The parents of the dead soldiers would draw the blinds in respect for their sons.

Development

- Students should work out that after four years of fighting, Sassoon and the soldiers are feeling elated, relieved and glad the war has ended. We should 'feel' his happiness.

- The choice of words might be singing/delight/freedom/beauty. He also compares his freedom from war with a caged bird that has been set free.

2 Explain and comment on authors' use of irony

Getting you thinking

You could also explain dramatic irony (when an audience knows something the characters in a play do not), perhaps giving the example of Duncan and Banquo in *Macbeth* commenting on the healthy air as they approach Macbeth's castle, where Duncan will be murdered.

How does it work?

There is humour in the metaphor 'shook the bottom out of all my Sunday school teachings', as if what he learned at Sunday school is a rusty bucket that just needs a good shake to ruin it. It is also funny that Twain's faith in morality is shaken by the fact that this boy was a 'sinner' ('notoriously worldly') yet has been rewarded – or so it seems – by God.

Now you try it

Encourage students to notice especially:

- Swift's tone in phrases such as 'of my acquaintance', 'most delicious, nourishing, and wholesome food' and 'humbly offer it to public consideration'. How formal or informal is this? What attitude to his reader does he seem to have?

- The phrase 'persons of quality and fortune'. What would he actually think of wealthy people who ate children?

- What is especially ironic about his suggested advice to mothers and the words he uses for it?

- The phrase 'plump and fat for a good table'. What does it sound as if he is describing? In what sense is the table 'good'?

Development

It is outlandish to suggest that Irish babies should be eaten. However, *A Modest Proposal* gets at the fact that something has to be done about Irish poverty. By using irony, Swift brings attention to the problem Ireland faced.

It is worth pointing out to students that some people did not realise Swift was using irony and took him seriously. They thought he really was suggesting that Irish babies should be eaten!

3 Analyse how writers use different sentence structures and rhythms

Getting you thinking

Encourage students in this lesson to 'hear' the rhythms that different sentences create: for example, short and sharp; balanced between two viewpoints; winding and sinuous with lots of caveats and subordinate clauses.

Now you try it

Remind students of the definitions of simple, compound and complex sentences.

- **Simple:** a single complete clause containing a subject and a verb. (Example: He rushed home.)

- **Compound:** two simple sentences joined with 'and', 'or', 'but' or 'yet'. (Examples: *He rushed home and found his mother asleep. He rushed home but was still late for dinner.*)

- **Complex:** one or more clauses often joined by conjunctions such as 'because', 'however', 'when', 'where', etc. One clause will be the main clause (*he rushed home*), while the other(s) adds extra information to the sentence and is therefore subordinate to the main clause. (Example: *Because he was already late, he rushed home, only to find she had already gone*.)

Explain to students that in this passage, Orwell uses a combination of **simple**, **compound** and **complex** sentences in a rhythmical way. He often begins a new subject – and a new paragraph – with a short sentence that sets out the subject of the paragraph. In this case, it is 'In January there came bitterly hard weather.' This fact leads to there being a lot of meetings, in which Snowball and Napoleon (two of the pigs in charge) clash.

The next sentence is a little longer. It is a compound sentence, made by joining two short sentences with 'and'. The next sentence, another compound sentence, is longer still.

Then comes a complex sentence with a **subordinate clause**: 'who were manifestly cleverer than the other animals'. (The sentence would work grammatically without this subordinate clause: 'It had come to be accepted … that the pigs should decide all questions of farm policy.') Slipping the idea of the pigs' intelligence into the sentence like this cleverly hints at the way in which the pigs themselves have led the other animals to regard them as the natural leaders of the farm.

Development

1 Ask students to reflect on their reading of the speech:

- Do students notice a different kind of pause when a semicolon, as opposed to a comma, is used?

- Which parts of the sentence would they emphasise if they were performing it for real?

- Are there any individual words they would stress?

- Do students think the sentence structures work well in the speech?

- Do they notice any other effective features (such as repetitions building to a climax)?

2 Would the speech work better with simpler sentences? How does Elizabeth I try to appeal to her army?

4 Explore different kinds of dialogue in fiction

Getting you thinking

The students can work in pairs or small groups to answer the questions.

How does it work?

To comment on how this dialogue is natural but dramatically interesting, students need to see how it suggests character and relationships.

For example:

- Squid speaks to Stanley in a **jokey, ironic way**. This suggests that he takes a certain grim pleasure in knowing that Stanley won't have enjoyed his first hole one bit.

- But when Stanley **groans, the boys laugh**. This suggests that there is a sort of camaraderie between them. It is as if they are part of a club and Stanley has just joined.

- X-Ray seems to be the leader of the group. This is suggested by the way Squid **backs him up**, saying 'That's right.'

- The boys have quite a tough attitude to their situation, and perhaps enjoy thinking that Stanley has to go through what they have gone through already. X-Ray seems to want to make Stanley expect the worst. He certainly doesn't try to cheer him up.

- The boys speak **informally**: 'no way', 'kid'. Note that Americans use 'Don't lie to me' and 'Am I right?' as jokey, informal expressions.

Now you try it

This passage is from 'Strike-Pay' by D.H. Lawrence.

Try to draw out from students why the writer might have chosen to use dialect in his characters' speech. Does the narrator of the story speak in the same way? Why did he choose not to use dialect in the narration of the story? Would they find it difficult to read a whole story or poem in a particular dialect? Have they read any stories or poems that do do this? What did they think of this?

Development

Students may find these terms useful for their essay: formal, informal, naturalistic, colloquial, dialogue, narrative, telling, showing.

5 Compare how writers use descriptive language in different texts

Now you try it

Go over the answers to the questions with students:

1

Lee	Durrell
each blade tattooed with tiger-skins (see)	crab-like spiders (see)
chirped/chattered (hear)	growling fatly … (hear)
rank with dark odours (smell)	

2 Lee creates humour by seeing things from the point of view of a small boy, the grass being taller than him.

3 Durrell gives animals human characteristics: ladybirds are 'rotund and amiable', the humming-bird hawk-moths are fussily efficient.

4 Durrell was a naturalist and gives a closer description of wildlife. Students should find plenty of examples.

Development

Pupils should work in pairs on this exercise. They can write down the reasons for their choice and then justify their decisions to the whole group.

Chapter 5 AF6 Identify and comment on writers' purposes and viewpoints, and the overall effect of the text on the reader

1 Use detailed evidence from a text to identify the writer's purpose (Part 1)

Getting you thinking

Ask the class whether they think the painter had the same intention in his painting.

Students should notice that 'the damsel in distress' likes the dragon. She finds him 'nicely physical' with a 'sexy tail'. She does not fancy the boy and she wonders if he has acne, blackheads and/or bad breath. However, she is pragmatic and so goes along with the boy.

The poet is making us rethink assumptions that girls are sweet, passive, bound to fall in love with their 'rescuer' and objects of love and quest – rather than real girls with their own opinions and feelings. She's not even faithful to the dragon: 'a girl's got to think of her future'. The poet questions how women are presented in legend and history by giving this one a surprising voice. Whether the painting is questioning – or promoting – the pale, passive virgin stereotype is a matter of opinion. But the humour comes from the way this painting of the legend is usually 'read': as a damsel in distress.

Now you try it

Medieval knights were nobles – upper class (in the sense of being born into a noble family) but also supposedly 'noble' in the sense of being virtuous and well behaved. Villeins – peasants – were assumed to be 'villains'.

Ask students if they think the painter intended his St George to seem noble?

Development

Students should identify the following:

- The girl questions whether she wants to be rescued.

- She knows the dragon likes her and she finds him sexy.

- In contrast, she does not fancy her rescuer but she is pragmatic.

- St George appears arrogant, 'you couldn't do better than me at the moment.'

- St George asks the girl why she is going against 'sociology and myth' and tells her she has no choice. His will prevails, 'does it matter what you want?'

2 Use detailed evidence from a text to identify the writer's purpose (Part 2)

Getting you thinking

Allow students to explore their own ideas. See how many different ideas the group can come up with, then ask them to justify their ideas.

Again, allow students to report their findings to the class as a whole.

Explain to students that this painting is a portrait of Giovanni di Nicolao Arnolfini and his wife Giovanna Cenami by Jan van Eyck. Arnolfini was an affluent merchant living in Bruges in Belgium.

How does it work?

Lots of people think the picture in the mirror shows the artist himself. He might have included himself to show he was a friend of the wealthy couple and to add to his status, or he might just have been having fun.

Development

An artist uses detail and clues in their paintings to build a picture that conveys their purpose. A writer uses words, sentences and paragraphs to build a whole text which fulfils their purpose.

Students can use visual aids such as PowerPoint or a poster if they wish.

Listeners should make sure that they give feedback on the following points:

● Has the speaker looked carefully at the image and come up with his or her own ideas about the artist's purpose?

● Has the speaker given detailed evidence for his or her ideas?

Extension

For homework, students could find a picture they like and explain what they think it is about.

3 Give detailed evidence for your opinions at word, sentence and text levels

Getting you thinking

Allow students to work in pairs and then choose a few pairs to report back to the class.

Now you try it

Remind students that the book will be aimed at a wide range of people, not just one type.

How does it work?

The blurb writer's main purpose is to sell the book, by making it sound knowledgeable, comprehensive and reliable. You need to give detailed evidence for this opinion, finding and explaining words and phrases like 'first hand accounts', 'complete guide' and 'expert insights' to support your ideas.

Development

Students may want to use the following paragraph or sentence starters:

The purpose of this text is…
The text targets…
It appeals to this audience by…
This would attract these readers because…
In conclusion, I think that…

4 Explain writers' viewpoints using detailed textual evidence

Getting you thinking

Students should point out that:

1 ● She is a school girl, and wears a blue and white uniform.
   ● Her hair is golden and she wears plaits.
   ● She looks like a painting.
   ● She has fine sweat on her forehead.

2 ● She is young.
   ● She is seen as important/perfect.
   ● She is seen as angelic.
   ● This could be an important moment in the girl's life.

- He has a 'hunger' for her.
- He could be shy, 'trembling to recite her name'.

Development

Ask students if they can work out how the girl feels, using implied meaning from the text.

Is she laughing at the boy? Are her companions joining in? Or is she laughing at something else?

5 Understand a text's effect on the reader and explain how the writer has created it

Getting you thinking

You could ask students to undertake the following:

1 Examine the collection of images you have created. What impression does this picture give you of the place Walcott is describing?

2 What picture is created of Tobago in the middle of summer in the first seven lines?

   Is it

   - hectic or slow-paced
   - crowded or spacious
   - lively or sleepy
   - rapidly changing
   - something else?

3 Now think about how the poet has used punctuation in these lines.

   To develop an active response to reading and the use of punctuation in the poem, you could ask students to:

   Stand up with a copy of the poem in your hands. Start reading the poem aloud. If you have lots of space, walk in a straight line while you read it. Every time there is a punctuation mark, turn 90°. Always turn in the same direction.

   When you have read up to 'August', stop and do the whole thing again.

4 Answer these questions:

   a What did you notice about the punctuation in the first four lines?

   b What did you notice about the punctuation in the last three lines that you read?

   c How did this make you read them differently?

How does it work?

Allow the students to read the poem several times. Then ask them to look at the question – What do these images tell you about the place Walcott is describing?

Here is a possible Level 6 answer.

The poet describes 'sun-stoned beaches' which suggests that in Tobago in midsummer it is very hot. The stones would be hard to touch and the intense sun would make the stones appear white.

The poet then uses colour as a contrast. The heat appears 'white', possibly through the glare of the sun. As a contrast, the river is 'green'. Green is a colour that suggests shade.

The palms in midsummer are 'yellow', like the sun's colour. They are also 'scorched', which means burnt and discoloured. This image suggests the place is so hot that the 'green' has gone from the palms.

In this hot weather, people sleep in summer houses. Here it is impossible to work in the hottest months. People are 'drowsing through August'.

The short, heavily end-stopped lines make the pace of the poem similarly slow and intense.

This response could be used as a 'crib' for teacher modelling of a written answer.

This is a good poem to exemplify to students that a range of responses are to be encouraged when analysing writing.

Development

The tone of the poem changes at the end and the images created are ones of regret. The poet has lived through days in Tobago – 'Days I have lost.' He has also changed – 'days that outgrow.'

The poet compares the past to daughters he once held in his 'harbouring arms'.

It is an interesting and unusual comparison. The poem, therefore, is about a place where Walcott once spent his time. He vividly remembers Tobago in midsummer. He appears to regret that those hot days are past and that they will never return. They are 'lost.'

Remind students that poets often write from a **first person** point of view, as if they are talking about their own feelings. However, we shouldn't assume that the narrator is the poet. Sometimes poets write from the point of view of a character in the first person and it is the character speaking, not the poet.

Development of the role of the persona in this poem would form a useful guided session for the more able.

1 Recognise textual conventions

Getting you thinking

Students should work out that the way snow is seen in this extract is unusual. It is mistaken for salt.

Now you try it

Explain to students that at the time many West Indians had been brought up to regard Britain as their mother country. Many had also fought for Britain in the Second World War. When Britain needed workers, the government offered a warm welcome and a voyage 'home' on a ship called the *Windrush*. However, the racist reception many West Indians received shocked them, and many experienced loneliness and isolation in their new life.

The place and the situation may well be familiar to students – the narrator describes watching the couples coming and going at a busy tube station near Piccadilly Circus.

Draw out with students that what is unusual and exciting about this narrative – particularly for its time – is the way it is written. Sam Selvon uses a West Indian English (sometimes called Jamaican patois or Creole) to tell the story of these new arrivals. Discuss with students how this can be seen both in the language used ('a sharp piece of skin') and the grammar of the narrative ('she give the ticket collector she ticket').

Ask students to work in pairs and to report back to the class.

2 Recognise how textual conventions can be combined to create a new literary form

This spread offers extra challenge to students working at and above Level 6.

Getting you thinking

Ask students to read the extract to themselves and discuss the question in pairs.

How does it work?

Show students how in news reporting or historical writing, the same 'story' would be told in different ways. For instance:

News: *The famous painting was removed at midnight on Sunday, and taken away for forensic examination by the police...*

History: *Duke Ferrara and his predecessors ruled for 900 years, establishing themselves as one of the most powerful Italian families, bringing to mind the Medicis or Borgia dynasties.*

A newspaper article would also have a headline about the murder and the wh- questions – who, when, where, what happened.

This, by contrast, is the narrative of a made-up person – a character – but arranged so that we see and understand more than he realises. It is literature.

Now you try it

One way of understanding the form is to say that it develops Shakespeare's soliloquies – where his characters 'think out loud' – into a mini-play with a story, character interplay and action of its own. It is meant to sound like actual speech, so is full of speech rhythms, the moods of a speaker who (as here) may be furious one minute and politely chattering the next. The dramatic monologue allows its writer to use the verse structure and sound effects of poetry.

Draw students' attention to the sinister repetition 'Looking as if she were alive … There she stands / As if alive', and the rapid, indirect and sinister summary of events 'This grew; I gave commands; / Then all smiles stopped together'.

Development

Encourage students to understand what **dramatic monologue** means.

1 The **narrative** is told to us in the present (as in a piece of drama).

2 Only **one** character speaks, so it is a **monologue** (*mono* = one, *logue* = speech (from the Greek word 'logos')). Although the Duke is having a conversation with someone else, we only hear his words. We have to work out what's happened – or is happening – from what he says and the gaps in his speech. It's a bit like hearing one side of a phone call where you have to imagine what the person on the other end is saying and doing.

If you think students will struggle to write about the Browning poem, you could show them the beginning of this funny modern dramatic monologue by E V Rieu about a visitor called 'Sir Smasham Uppe'.

> Good afternoon, Sir Smasham Uppe!
> We're having tea, do take a cup!
> Sugar and milk? Now let me see –
> Two lumps I think? Good gracious me!
> The silly thing slipped off your knee!
> Pray don't apologise, old chap
> A very trivial mishap!

They can answer the question in relation to this text instead.

More able students may enjoy tackling this question as an extension:

● What does this **new form** allow poets to do that previous forms could not?

3 Discuss how ideas are treated differently in different times and places

Getting you thinking

If students have access to the internet or the library, they can find out how William Wilberforce campaigned to end the slave trade in Britain.

How does it work?

Encourage students to read and engage with the Bill of Sale. What does it show us about the attitudes of the society and slave owners at the time?

Now you try it

● Do you know where – or how – your clothes were made?

Encourage students to understand that wherever their clothes were bought, there is a good chance that they were made in Third World sweatshops by low-paid (near-slave) workers, often women or very young children who we don't even think about. Instead, we think of how cool – or uncool – the clothes are, or how cleverly bought in a 'sale'.

Students interested in this topic might enjoy reading *Iqbal* by Francesco D'Adamo. This book tells the real-life story of Iqbal Masih, a former child slave who campaigned against child labour in Pakistan until his assassination in 1995. It is believed he was murdered by those hostile to his work for the Bonded Labor Liberation Front.

Development

● Students should work out that attitudes to texts change over time because society's values and attitudes are not constant.

● There may be a variety of answers from the students. However, ask students if texts from previous times should be read today, so that we can understand history better. Reading texts from previous times should give us a better understanding of where we came from and who we are today.

4 Discuss how racism in texts is read differently in different times and places

Getting you thinking

The word in square brackets, 'slaves', replaces the word 'Niggers' in Twain's original text. The word is repeated endlessly throughout the novel, not as any great statement but as a casual and accepted everyday term (in the book and the society). If appropriate, you can share this information with the class. Does it change their attitude to the book at all? Students may be interested to know that there has been a long-running debate in the US about whether the novel is suitable to be studied in schools.

How does it work?

The extract is a great description of boyish mischief. And only Tom, not Huck, plays the trick. But Huck's colloquial American South narrative (as written by the author Mark Twain) mocks Jim's African beliefs: '[Slaves] is always talking about witches in the dark by the kitchen fire'. If Tom plays a trick on Jim physically, you could say that the author makes fun of him in the narrative.

Not because Mark Twain was racist. (Although his character Tom acts in a very superior manner towards Jim, Tom is not approved of by the author, nor is he the hero of this book. Huck befriends Jim and they run away together. They are both seeking freedom from 'sivilisation' and live as equals.) But Mark Twain's society – in which slavery had only recently been abolished – certainly was racist. And his story was set in the American South of the 1830s, when slavery was still in full force.

Now you try it

- According to the Nazi stereotype promoted in German schools Jews were bad. They had 'hook noses and blue chins'.
- The boy sees the Jew as an old man with white hair, no different from any other old man in Germany.
- He feels guilty, sees the other boys as 'cool' and sees himself as 'a disapproving old woman.' However, he walks home alone, which suggests that he knows deep within himself that what the other boys are doing is wrong.

Development

Ask students to work in pairs to compare how the racism of the two societies is presented. They should focus, in particular, on the attitudes of the main characters in each and write up their discussion, answering the following questions:

- Do you think either character realises his society is racist?
- Does either character seem to feel uncomfortable about what others are doing in the story?

5 Discuss how the same literary form is used differently in different times

Getting you thinking

Begin by asking students: would they rather have a sonnet written in a Valentine's card – or a limerick? Why? Draw out that limericks are traditionally joke poems, usually rude. If you're serious about love, you wouldn't send a limerick. You'd send a sonnet.

Students can read the passage from *Romeo and Juliet* on p.21 of this book.

Feed back students' ideas, drawing out these suggested answers to question 2 of the activity:

- Lines 1–8: her beauty is more lovely, more reliable, not so changeable and longer lasting

than an English summer (lines 1–4); not (like summer) too hot, or cloudy, or subject to change or decline (lines 5–8).

- Lines 9–14: her beauty will age and die but in his poem ('eternal lines') it will last forever.

Ask students to look at the use of rhyme and punctuation in the poem. Do they notice any patterns? There are definite sections marked by strong punctuation. Lines 5–8 repeat the ideas of lines 1–4 in a different way. Do lines 9–12 (beginning with that 'But') repeat the idea? Or do they say something new? If so, do they fit better with the ideas of lines 13–14?

Explain to students that before Shakespeare, the **convention** was that a sonnet divided at the end of line 8. But, in this one, lines 9–12 are separated from lines 13–14. Lines 9–12 do repeat the idea given in lines 1–4 and 5–8: her beauty is better than summer. But lines 9–12 also take the idea forward towards the final idea of lines 13–14: 'thy eternal summer shall not fade'. Shakespeare is **developing** the **conventions** of the English sonnet.

How does it work?

Explain that Shakespeare wrote many sonnets. Allow students to research and find other English sonnets. They can look in the library or use the internet.

Development

Remind students that

- writers rarely invent completely new literature (Petrarch did – but even he partly based his sonnet on a Persian love poem called a ghazal, which is a poetic form usually consisting of rhyming couplets and a refrain.)
- old forms gain new life from the new ways writers use them
- old forms (like words) can gain new meanings.

As an interesting exercise, allow students to have a go at writing a 14-line sonnet. This would make a good homework task.